David
VOLUME 2

Encount... ...od's heart

MICHAEL BENTLEY

SERIES EDITOR: SIMON J ROBINSON

DayOne

© Day One Publications 2007
First printed 2007

ISBN 978-1-84625-015-6

Unless otherwise indicated, Scripture quotations in this publication are from the Holy Bible: New International Version (NIV), copyright ©1973, 1978, 1984, International Bible Society. Used by permission of Hodder and Stoughton, a member of the Hodder Headline Group. All rights reserved.

British Library Cataloguing in Publication Data available

Published by Day One Publications
Ryelands Road, Leominster, HR6 8NZ
Telephone 01568 613 740   FAX 01568 611 473

email—sales@dayone.co.uk
web site—www.dayone.co.uk

All rights reserved
No part of this publication may be reproduced, or stored in a retrieval system, or transmitted, in any form or by any means, mechanical, electronic, photocopying, recording or otherwise, without the prior permission of Day One Publications.

Designed by Steve Devane and printed by Gutenberg Press, Malta.

FACE2FACE: **DAVID**

CONTENTS

1. Welcome your king — 6
2. Despising God's Holiness — 13
3. When you are angry with God — 21
4. Beware of despising the Lord — 29
5. When God says, 'No' — 36
6. How to pray — 42
7. God's free grace — 49
8. David's Foolish Night — 57
9. David's attempted cover up — 67
10. David's sin uncovered — 76
11. David's pardon from God — 85
12. Where has all the weeping gone? — 94
13. Suspended between heaven and earth — 105
14. A Traitor, a Cripple and a Very Old Man — 114
15. A costly offering — 123
16. Going Home — 133

FACE2FACE: **DAVID**

APPRECIATIONS

'In this volume Michael Bentley capably leads us through the years that King David reigned over all of Israel. David is one of the central figures of the entire Bible. It is crucial for us to have a good understanding of this great man. Michael Bentley does not let us down in providing that good understanding. He treats the life of David in a simple, straightforward fashion, never losing sight throughout of the practical significance of David for us and constantly holding before us David's greater Son, the Lord Jesus. A very good and satisfying book!'

Roger Ellsworth, Pastor of Immanuel Baptist Church, Benton, Illinois, USA and Bible commentator

'Michael Bentley has the gift of being able to refresh the familiar tales and breathe life into the old stories so that, once again, God's word becomes living and active and sharpens us to be more like our Saviour Jesus.'

Adrian Reynolds, Pastor-Teacher, Yateley Baptist Church

'Michael Bentley is a preacher and has a heart for preaching and for other preachers. This comes through powerfully in his book which is full of wisdom from the life of David and which brings to life the story of David in a way that we can use today. If you are a preacher, teacher or small group leader, this book will provide you with many expository nuggets to use to guide people into further maturity in Christ.'

Chris Porter, Minister, Easthampstead Baptist Church, Bracknell

Dedication

To Isabella Rose Bentley (born 27th November 2006) and her sisters, Anais and Talia Bentley (in New Zealand), her cousins, Daniel, Benjamin and Amy Felts (in Kent, UK) and Alexander Underwood (in Bracknell, UK)

May these grandchildren of mine all grow up to be people after God's heart.

1 Welcome your king

2 Samuel 5:1–5

I remember our queen's coronation; it rained! Many thousands of people lined the route and huge numbers camped out all night by the roadside and the sales of cardboard periscopes rocketed as the people at the back of the pavements got ready to 'look over the heads' of those in front of them.

It was all on television, black and white of course. As we didn't own a set, my mum and I went to an older cousin of mine who owned one. In those days there were only two kinds, those with nine-inch screens or, if you could afford it, a twelve-inch version. It was a very exciting time. We could actually see the coronation as it happened, then within a few days we could see the whole thing in colour on the newsreels at the cinemas. The older people could remember the 1937 coronation of King George VI; in fact our town had a 'Coronation Clock' in the High Street which was donated at that time to commemorate the event.

In 2 Samuel 5 we have details of David's coronation. He had been anointed king many years before by the prophet Samuel, and later he had been acclaimed as king by the people of Judah. Now, many years later still 'all the tribes of

Israel came to David at Hebron' and acknowledged him as their king.

A PERSONAL RELATIONSHIP

People from all over the land came to David. Formerly Saul was king but he had spent many of his years hunting down and trying to kill David. However, the Lord had delivered David from Saul's hand, but now the former king was dead. Although many people were glad to be rid of Saul, David mourned his passing. David was sad particularly about the death of Saul's son, his dear friend Jonathan. David had lamented, 'I grieve for you, Jonathan, my brother; you were very dear to me. Your love for me was wonderful' (2 Samuel 1:26).

Since the death of Saul and Jonathan various children of Saul had tried to become king but none had succeeded because God had already chosen David to be king over the land. We might think we know what is best for us and our friends but God's plan and purpose for our lives is what matters more than anything else. We should all be seeking to live out God's purposes in our lives.

The elders from each of the tribes of Israel came to David and said, 'We are your own flesh and blood' (5:1) (i.e. they were all part of David's family). They all had the same father, Abraham. They had all sprung from the same forebears. They all worshipped the same God and they wanted David to be their leader. As they came to pay him homage David showed that he welcomed them as his brothers.

This picture reminds us of our Lord Jesus Christ. This is what he did for us, if we are his born-again people. 'In bringing many sons to glory, it was fitting that God, for whom and through whom everything exists, should make the author of their salvation perfect through suffering. Both the one who makes men holy and those who are made holy are of the same family. So Jesus is not ashamed to call them brothers' (Hebrews 2:10–11).

When these men came to David they were absolutely certain of what they wanted. 'They came to Hebron fully determined to make David king over all Israel' and there was no doubt in their mind that he was the one they wished to follow. Not only was he of the same family as themselves, but he was the one person they wanted to be king over them. 'All the rest of the Israelites were also of one mind to make David king' (1 Chronicles 12:38).

There had been some hesitancy earlier, but now they were united in wanting David as their king. We cannot hope to win our neighbourhood for Christ unless we and our fellow-Christians are united in our desire for evangelism. Disunity in a church, or among any people, is the greatest hindrance to progress. There must be love, joy and peace—and there must be a determination to put aside differences which may divide us. We must unite under one leader, the Lord Jesus Christ, and take our orders from him alone and the only place where we find those instructions is in the Bible, God's inerrant word.

A PROVEN TRACK RECORD

David had proved himself to the people and to God. He had made mistakes in the past and he was going to make many more in the future, but this did not alter the fact that he had proved himself to be a man after God's heart, in whom the Spirit of the Lord was clearly seen. First of all, David had confessed his sin to God and to those he had sinned against. When he did so, he discovered that God had freely forgiven him when he was truly contrite. Although he sometimes had to remain in the background for a while, he was eventually brought back to the word of the Lord. 'He who never makes mistakes never makes anything' is a popular and true saying, but David could rejoice in this: 'Blessed is he whose transgressions are forgiven, whose sins are covered. Blessed is the man whose sin the LORD does not count against him and in whose spirit there is no deceit' (Psalm 32:1–2).

David had led the people well in all their military campaigns. 'You were the one who led Israel' was how they viewed David. However, David knew that it was the Lord who had led them; nevertheless it was David who had the skill and courage to follow the leadings of God and go on and defeat their enemies. His natural talents had been brought under subjection to the Holy Spirit and those abilities had been fine-tuned by spiritual gifts.

Such gifts are meant to be used for God's glory. In 1933 the late Gracie Fields sang, 'I took my harp to a party but nobody asked me to play.' Sometimes Christians have God-given skills but the leaders in their churches never give them opportunity to exercise these because 'the pastor does everything'.

A DIVINE APPOINTMENT

The people reminded David that the Lord had said to him, 'You shall shepherd my people Israel' (5:2) even though God was their Shepherd. Psalm 100:3 says, 'Know that the LORD is God. It is he who made us, and we are his; we are his people, the sheep of his pasture.' Isaiah says, 'He tends his flock like a shepherd. He gathers the lambs in his arms and carries them close to his heart; he gently leads those that have young' (40:11). Micah also looks forward to the Messiah who will 'stand and shepherd his flock in the strength of the LORD' (Micah 5:4).

How does God shepherd his people? He uses under-shepherds, pastors and other church leaders. In the days of the Old Testament the king was the shepherd who was God's ordained leader of his people and he had various elders of the people to carry out his commands. David, who had spent all of his early life looking after sheep, would have been eminently qualified to lead the people.

But not only was David to be God's shepherd, he was to be his ruler as well. Who is worthy of such a tremendous task? Only a man in whom dwells the Spirit of God. Although David must often have felt unworthy, he accepted the challenge and allowed himself to be anointed as king over Israel (5:3). He knew that those whom God calls he also equips. He knew that God was with him and that he would help him carry out his weighty responsibilities.

A WONDERFUL KING

David proved to be one who would unite the whole nation. For the first time in their history they were all pulling in the same direction, at the same time. They were all bound up together as one nation under God, under David's leadership. Yet David was merely a foreshadowing of the one who would be called 'great David's greater Son'.

Jesus Christ is the only one who can bring all people together in unity. It is only as we come to the foot of Christ's cross and confess our sin that we can be accepted as one of his subjects and then he calls us to be his brothers and sisters. However, we must first repent of our sins, turn to him in faith and acknowledge our allegiance to his cause.

Christ has been anointed our shepherd and our ruler. He is God's chosen servant and he now reigns in heaven. Listen to the words of Abner when he conferred with the elders of Israel a few years before this, 'For some time you have wanted to make David your king. Now do it' (2 Samuel 3:17–18). God calls us all to act in the same way in our allegiance to the Lord Jesus Christ.

FOR FURTHER STUDY

1. Study the conflict between the house of Saul and the house of David in 2 Samuel 3 and 4 and especially note 2 Samuel 3:1.
2. Study the following Scriptures and note the importance of loyalty to the Lord and our fellow-believers—Genesis 39:22–23; 2 Kings 12:15; Nehemiah 7:2; 1 Corinthians 4:17; Hebrews 3:2, 5; Revelation 2:13.
3. Notice the importance of unity among God's people (see 2 Chronicles 30:12; Psalm 133; John 17:23; Romans 15:5; Ephesians 4:3; Colossians 3:14).

TO THINK ABOUT AND DISCUSS

1. Think about an important task you have been called to perform—perhaps promotion to a more responsible position in your company. What kind of skills did you need to motivate those in your team to produce the work necessary for the company to progress?

2. *Share some experiences which you have had where you have been asked to tell lies for the company or otherwise compromise your Christian faith.*

3. *How would you seek to encourage unity in a church or congregation where there is a large measure of disagreement and hostility?*

2 Despising God's holiness

2 Samuel 6:1–7

Are there occasions when you feel especially holy and so blessed that you have a strong desire to dedicate the whole of your life to God? When that happens to us we experience a warm glow of satisfaction and we feel especially holy.

In T. S. Eliot's *Murder in the Cathedral* there is a moment when Thomas à Becket, Archbishop of Canterbury, is wondering what he should do despite many temptations. He muses, 'Now is my way clear, now is the meaning plain; Temptation shall not come in this kind again. The last temptation is the greatest treason: To do the right deed for the wrong reason.'[1]

Sometimes we are like that; we do the right thing for the wrong reason and at other times our motives are good but our methods are wrong. That was exactly David's position here. His desire was right but he went about things in the wrong way.

DAVID HAD A GOOD HEART
For far too long the ark of God had not held a central position in Israel. For many years it had stayed in Kiriath Jearim

(Baalah of Judah). All during the reign of Saul it had been hidden away and it had lain forgotten. Ever since the Philistines had returned it after they had captured it from the Israelites it had been neglected (1 Samuel 4:11).

Originally the ark was the centre of worship in the tabernacle. God had given clear instructions regarding its construction, and its purpose was to symbolize the presence of the Lord in the midst of his people. It had a golden lid which was God's throne and side by side on the lid sat two golden cherubim (angels). The ark was a gold-covered box in which lay Aaron's rod, a golden pot of manna and the two tablets containing the Ten Commandments which had been written by the finger of God (Exodus 31:18).

Yet for about fifty years this symbol of God's presence had been neglected and stored seven and a half miles south-west of Jerusalem. It was no surprise then that the Israelites had been passing through many trials. They had abandoned the sign of God's presence and no-one enquired of the Lord all during the long reign of King Saul (1 Chronicles 13:3).

When anyone forgets the Lord God Almighty then they are certain to suffer sooner or later. David knew this, so as soon as he had captured Jerusalem and set up his kingdom in that city his desire was to rectify the wrongs of the past. He wanted to take some action that would remind the people that God was with them so he erected a special tent where the ark could be placed (6:17). He then made preparations for bringing it from the home of Abinadab to Jerusalem (6:3).

He chose 30,000 men to accompany the procession (6:1). Perhaps he selected this number because 30,000 foot soldiers had been killed when the Philistines captured the ark from them (1 Samuel 4:10). He also spoke respectfully of it and called it 'the ark of God, which is called by the Name, the name of the LORD Almighty, who is enthroned between the cherubim that are on the ark' (6:2). He and the whole house of Israel were anticipating the time when it would be especially honoured (6:5). It was placed right in the centre of the procession in glorious splendour, and it rested on a new cart which had been built especially for the occasion.

David had spared no expense in showing everyone that he wanted to give glory to God. He desired to demonstrate that the ark was worthy of being transported on the very finest of vehicles. He wanted it to have a smooth, swift and efficient means of transport from the home of Abinadab (which was on a hill) to the glorious tent in Jerusalem (which was on an even more important hill).

Great joy and singing accompanied the procession and all kinds of musical instruments were used to glorify the name of the Lord—such as those named in Psalm 150. Everything went very smoothly until they came to the threshing-floor of Nacon. At this point the oxen who were pulling the ark stumbled. This was a very serious thing but Uzzah, one of Abinadab's sons, acted quickly and sensibly. He stretched out his hand and steadied it. This young man no doubt was demonstrating that he cared for the ark. He did not want to see it fall off the cart and be damaged. He was doing the intelligent thing by exercising foresight and lending God a hand. Yet the astonishing thing was that God saw this action as an irreverent one and struck him down 'and he died there before the ark of God' (6:7).

On the face of it this is one of the most puzzling stories in the whole Bible. Uzzah performed a kind and helpful act, yet he was punished for it. He had, presumably, been put in this position by David with the main intention of seeing that the ark remained safely on the cart. Yet when he stretched out his hand to steady it, he was struck dead. Why was that?

DAVID USED A WRONG METHOD

Although David's intention had been honourable, he had forgotten God's clear instructions which had said that the ark of the Lord was holy. In Numbers 4 there are detailed instructions about how it should be treated and its contents venerated. Firstly, the ark was so sacred that no human beings were to look into it lest they defile it by their sinfulness. Numbers 4:20 tells us that 'the Kohathites (those detailed to carry the ark) must not look at the holy things, even for a moment, or they will die'. These instructions were still in force in 1 Samuel 6:19 at the time that 'God struck down some of the men of Beth Shemesh, putting seventy of them to death *because they looked into the ark of the LORD*'. We see, then, that God does mean what he says. We should never treat anything that the Bible says in a light or flippant fashion.

Secondly, we are told that when the ark was moved it was to be covered. There is no mention of David's doing so on this occasion. We should be careful of drawing conclusions from the silences in the Bible however moving the ark was an important matter and David gives us plenty of detail about other things in connection with its transportation.

Thirdly, when the tabernacle (the forerunner of the temple) was set up the Lord said that only the Kohathites (a branch of the priestly tribe of Levi) were to move the holy things. In

Numbers 4:15 we read, 'When the camp is ready to move, the Kohathites are to come and do the carrying.' Then this stern warning is given, 'But they must not touch the holy things *or they will die.*'

Everyone who took the trouble to find out what God had said about moving the ark would have known this. So we see from the story of Uzzah that not only does God keep his promise, he also fulfils his threats. He is a very foolish person who only takes notice of the promises of God's blessings. We must remember that the word of God declares not only that 'he who believes has everlasting life' (John 6:47), but also 'the soul who sins is the one who will die' (Ezekiel 18:4).

A fourth stipulation was that it should be carried using poles. There were special rings at each corner of the ark and every time it was to be moved, poles were to be placed through these rings so that the Kohathites could carry it carefully.

We can see then why Uzzah had to die. He had ignored God's dire warnings about the handling of holy things. He thought he was helping God. He used his intelligence and so steadied the ark to stop it from falling to the ground. In other words, he put his own reasoning before the teaching of God's word. When anyone does this they are in danger. One of the reasons that the church is so weak today is that human thinking has been given a higher status than God's word. People reason, 'Miracles can't happen, so there must be some mistakes in the Bible manuscripts.' They want to elevate human thinking to a higher plane than the teaching of God's word.

How sad it is that a great man like David thought he could improve on God's word. He had forgotten the teaching of

Numbers because he had been so taken up with his own kingly glory.

This is possibly how David thought, 'A cart would be preferable to men carrying the ark on poles. The instructions given by Moses would be seen as an old-fashioned way of doing things in these sophisticated days. If I make a brand-new cart especially for this occasion then people will realize that only the best is good enough for God.' David wanted the ark to have a much more dignified journey than if men had carried it on their shoulders by means of poles. Perhaps he reasoned that the Kohathites were no longer needed and as the Philistines had moved the ark on a cart, also a new cart (1 Samuel 6:7), no harm had come to them, so the Israelites would be safe also.

However, this kind of thinking shows us how foolish it is to follow the methods of the world. If we do so, we are doomed to failure. This means we must be careful how we present the gospel message so that it appeals to the unsaved masses. Nothing outside of the simple preaching of the gospel should be attempted without first of all bathing it in much prayer and thought and godly discussion.

A final question to ask is, 'What made the oxen stumble?' We do not know, but this is certain: we will surely stumble if we ignore God's clear instructions and despise his holiness.

SOME LESSONS FOR TODAY

We should remember that God's word is never out-of-date. He is eternal and it abides for ever. We must not say of clear Bible teaching, 'That doesn't apply today' or 'The Bible doesn't mean that.'

We should also remember that any action, however right it

may seem, should not be carried out without much prayer. In 1 Chronicles 13:1 David consulted with each of his officers and commanders to see whether they thought it was right to take the ark to Jerusalem. But there is no mention of his consulting the Lord.

FOR FURTHER STUDY

1. Outline the teaching in Numbers 4:1–20 as it pertains to the ark of God.
2. Why is holiness important? (See Psalm 18:26; Proverbs 15:26; Habakkuk 1:13; Matthew 5:8; 1 Peter 1:15).
3. Consider what happened to these Bible characters when they disobeyed the Lord's command—Moses in Numbers 20:2, 11, 24; Saul in 1 Samuel 28:17–18; Jonah in Jonah 1:2–3.

TO THINK ABOUT AND DISCUSS

1. How should we behave, knowing that God is present with us at all times? Discuss the things that were shunned by Christians in other generations but are now considered to be acceptable—e.g. drinking alcohol, enjoying the cinema, going to pubs and wearing casual clothes at church services.
2. What criteria should we use to decide whether a method of evangelism is out of date?
3. Share examples of a time you received God's guidance after praying about it. Were there other times when you forgot to pray about a decision that had to be made. What happened?

FACE2FACE: **DAVID**

Notes

1 **T. S. Eliot,** *The Complete Poems and Plays of T. S. Eliot* (London: Faber and Faber, 1975), p. 258.

3 When you are angry with God

2 Samuel 6:8–15

Uncontrolled anger is a frightening thing. When a husband comes home the worse for drink and he finds that his meal is not waiting for him he can fall into the most terrible rage. Sometimes his befuddled mind accepts that he has spent too much time and far too much money on alcohol and he realizes that his wife is going to be very upset with him. In his bewildered state his immediate reaction is to go on the offensive and shout and scream at her. He loses his temper to cover up his own wrong.

It is said that 'anger is an acid that can do more harm to the vessel in which it is stored than to anything on which it is poured' and 'anger is just one letter short of danger'. The great Greek mathematician Pythagoras said, 'Anger begins in folly and ends in repentance.' An antidote to anger is to remember that the one thing that improves the longer it is kept is our temper.

DAVID WAS ANGRY WITH GOD

David had decided to move the ark of the covenant to Jerusalem but he had ignored, or forgotten, God's clear instructions concerning its transportation. Only members of the tribe of Levi should move it; it should only be carried on poles and under no circumstances should anyone touch this symbol of God's presence; it was holy. However, David did not have the ark carried; he moved it on a cart, on a new one especially made for it, but when the oxen pulling the cart stumbled, Uzzah put out his hand to prevent it from falling to the ground. This resulted in his death.

To us this seems to be a cruel and heartless act from an ungrateful God and we find it difficult to understand why Uzzah should be punished for doing such a sensible and seemingly God-honouring act. However, the lesson is that if we do things in our own way, rather than following God's revealed pattern, then we are in for trouble.

We can sympathize with David in his anger at God. We too find it difficult to accept why he can take from us by death someone who is in the prime of life and a pillar in society, while evil men are allowed to live to a great age. We grieve over the death of innocent young children who are killed in wars and we find it difficult to understand why God allows these awful things to happen.

Why was David angry with God? He was upset because his own plans had been thwarted. He had decided that the ark should be taken to his new headquarters in Jerusalem. There he had built a special tent for it and he had let all the people know that a great procession would take place in honour of this event. But now, by killing Uzzah, God had spoiled his plans.

Even though David then named the place Perez Uzzah (the outbreak against Uzzah) he was probably angry more because he had been made to look a fool than because one of his men had been killed. Much later in the story we find that David had come to his senses and admitted that the real problem was because he had not enquired of the Lord how he should move the ark (see 1 Chronicles 15:13). We should never be surprised if things go wrong when we leave God out of our thinking. We must ensure that we do more than make our plans and then seek God's blessing on them. We must seek God's will first. The Bible is full of principles which should guide us through life. God desires to bless us and he wants to guide us and help us, but he does demand that we do things in his way. Furthermore, God's way does not change. The circumstances may alter but God's word and his truth abide for ever.

David's pride had been dented. He was the great King David! He had been specially chosen by God to lead this nation. He had been anointed by the prophet Samuel many years before (1 Samuel 16:13). He had proved himself in battle many times. He had been a godly leader, despite many difficulties, but now with the death of Uzzah he would be seen as a failure, especially when it was realized that he had ignored the clear teaching of God's word. David was humiliated before all the people. Everyone had seen what had happened, or they would soon hear about it. He must have thought that his status as king had diminished in the eyes of all the people and so would have wondered how he could lift up his head among them in the future.

How often it is that we, as Christian people, feel ourselves to be failures. This especially applies to those who are leaders in a church or home group. We feel that we cannot continue with our service for the Lord because we have let him down. The writer of Psalm 42 knew this same feeling of humiliation when he wrote, 'My tears have been my meat day and night, while men say to me all day long, "Where is your God?"' (Psalm 42:3). When trouble comes to one of God's servants, the people of the world are very quick to call out, 'Where is your God now?'

DAVID'S ANGER TURNED TO JOY

The next stage in David's emotions was about to start. Instead of being angry with God, he started to be afraid of him (6:9). Almost in frustration he called out, 'How can the ark of the LORD ever come to me?' Because of all the upset he was not willing to take the ark into Jerusalem. He was sad because of all that had happened but it seems that he was also convicted of his sin, so much so that he did not feel worthy to house the ark. All the while we have unconfessed sin in our hearts we have good cause to be afraid of God.

Because he did not know what to do, David put the ark in the home of Obed-Edom and during the three months it was there the Lord blessed Obed-Edom and his entire household. Eventually David heard about this blessing which God had brought upon all those who lived with Obed-Edom. It is always newsworthy when God rains down his blessing upon an individual or family.

The blessing came to him because the ark symbolized God's presence. This scene reminds us that when we have the Lord Jesus Christ living in the centre of our lives and our families then we can be sure of his blessing. We can hope that the way we live our lives will be noted by our neighbours, and that it will have an effect on them.

Thinking about these things, David was even more convinced that he should have the ark dwelling within his new capital city of Jerusalem. In 1 Chronicles 15 we read that he summoned the Levites to him and instructed them to move the ark, only this time it was to be moved in the way that the Lord had laid down in Numbers. He acknowledged that the trouble had come because the Levites did not bring up the ark of the Lord, the God of Israel, in the prescribed manner (see 1 Chronicles 15:12–13).

Now we see a great change coming over David. Once he had confessed his sin he became very humble and was reconciled to God. He could then join in a joyful procession to the city of Jerusalem. No-one can celebrate the blessings of God if sin dwells in their hearts. Before anything else happens this sin must be confessed and dealt with.

This time the procession moved forward and after it had taken just six steps David sacrificed a bull and a fatted calf. This seems strange behaviour to us but David needed to do it. Probably the sacrifice had a two-fold significance. It was to make atonement for his past sin but also it was a thanksgiving that God had forgiven him and he was now able to bring the ark to his own city.

Christ's sacrificial death on Calvary had not then taken place, so David had to offer an animal sacrifice to cover his sin. We are now privileged to live in the age of grace, knowing that Christ has shed his precious blood on the cross to cleanse us from every stain of sin.

David could only take a joyful part in this procession by first learning that his sins had been forgiven. His anger had been taken away and he had stopped being afraid of God; he had been reconciled to him and was looking forward to having the blessing of God's presence with him in his own city. David was so happy that he danced before the Lord with all his might

(6:14). He was happy because he was now, finally, doing God's will. He laid aside his royal robes and danced in a simple tunic. He wanted to show everyone that he was God's servant. 'Only a monarch as humble in heart and lovely in spirit as David could ever have achieved such a spiritual triumph. On this occasion God took great delight in coming to dwell among his chosen people.'[1]

WHEN WE ARE ANGRY WITH GOD

We become angry with God when things do not work out as we want them to do. In that case we should humbly accept that God knows what is best for us. We should examine our lives, our motives and our desires to see whether there is anything selfish about our attitude to God and to other people, and we should seek to put these things right. This is what David did. He discovered what he had been doing that was wrong. He confessed it to the Lord and he made sure that he behaved correctly in the future.

We become angry when our pride is hurt. Sometimes in these cases God brings chastisement upon us so that we will come to our senses. He never allows things to go wrong for us merely because he wants us to suffer. Instead he often uses difficulties to show us what is wrong in our lives and to encourage us to put matters right. The Bible says, 'My son, do not make light of the Lord's discipline, and do not lose heart when he rebukes you, because the Lord disciplines those he loves' (Hebrews 12:5–6).

At other times God sends trouble in our way to break our proud spirits. In 1 Peter 5:6 we are commanded, 'Humble yourselves, therefore, under God's mighty hand, that he may lift you up in due time.' God is calling us to repent of our anger against him and the teaching of his word. It is as though he is saying to us, 'I know you get angry sometimes, and on occasions that is understandable, but in your anger I want you to make sure that you do not sin' (Ephesians 4:26). None of us should ever let anger fester; we should deal with it before we go to bed that night. Paul tells us not to 'let the sun go down while [we] are still angry' (Ephesians 4:26).

In all our anger we must ensure that we do not 'give the devil a foothold' (Ephesians 4:27). Satan is going to do his best to make us dwell on our anger instead of turning to God's word. We should heed the words of James, 'My dear brothers, take note of this: Everyone should be quick to listen, slow to speak, and slow to become angry, for man's anger does not bring about the righteous life that God desires' (James 1:19–20). The Lord wants us to live in a right relationship with himself and also with other people.

FOR FURTHER STUDY

1. Notice how many verses in the Bible ask, 'Why do the wicked prosper?' (See Job 21:7–15; Psalm 73:3–5,12; Ecclesiastes 7:15; Habakkuk 1:13).
2. Then see how God answers these charges. (See Psalm 37:1, 8–10; Psalm 73:18–20, 27–28).

TO THINK ABOUT AND DISCUSS

1. Consider the teachings that James gives in regard to the right and wrong uses of our tongues in James 3:1–12.

2. Discuss how we should control what we say and how we can act with humility (see James 3:13–18).

3. How should Christians act when our honest behaviour seems to achieve nothing, while those who cheat and lie (under the pretence that this is normal business behaviour) appear to prosper?

4. Think of a situation where you have 'lost out' by being honest. Share with others the feelings you experienced and explain how God gave you the grace to cope in those difficult circumstances.

Notes

1 Phillip Keller, *David the Shepherd King* (Word Publishing, 1986), p. 56.

4 Beware of despising the Lord

2 Samuel 6:16–23

Many years ago, while on a visit to one of the seaside towns in the south of England, I remember looking up and seeing the face of an elderly woman looking down on all the activity below. She seemed sad and worried but, above all, she gave the impression of being very, very lonely.

In this chapter we find a lonely woman, sitting on her balcony watching a procession from her window. She had no part in this parade; she was merely an onlooker. She was Michal, Saul's daughter, and David's wife.

WHAT DID MICHAL OBSERVE?

She saw a great throng of joyful people who were rejoicing because they were bringing the ark of the Lord into Jerusalem. The hope was that this ark would bring God's blessing to the kingdom. We read, 'The entire house of Israel brought up the ark of the LORD with shouts and the sound of trumpets' (6:15). Everyone was excited at the prospect of the ark's finally residing in the special tent that David had erected for it in his capital city. It may not have been customary for the women to join the procession; we can imagine that they gathered in groups to enjoy as much of the fun as they could. Even the slave girls watched with pleasure at these events.

But Michal was apparently sitting alone, watching all these things from a window. She was separated from everyone else and she frowned as she saw David leaping and dancing 'before the LORD'. She had been deeply in love with her husband (1 Samuel 18:20) and had risked her life by rescuing him from his enemies (1 Samuel 18:12) but now she saw David in an entirely different light. It seems that her love for him had grown cold. Earlier in their married life she could have forgiven him almost anything. Once she would have admired him for going down among the people and mixing with them, but now she could only find fault with him. Everything that he said and did filled her with hatred.

This is what happens to anyone when their marriage begins to go sour. 'I can't do a thing right,' is what a partner will say in these circumstances. It is the same with a believer and his or her relationship with God. When we first become Christians the Lord Jesus Christ is the 'altogether lovely' one (Song of Solomon 5:16), but when we begin to drift away from him then our love grows cold. When we were new Christians meeting others for worship was something that we prized very highly, but when we backslide we lose our joy and everything becomes pointless. We are still united with Christ in salvation, but there is a barrier between us and the Lord. In this state we tend to find fault with everyone in the church fellowship. The prayer meetings no longer hold any warmth and Sunday worship seems meaningless. We even begin to despise those things that once we felt were very precious.

As Michal looked at the procession she did not see David dancing before the Lord; all she noticed was her husband making a fool of himself. She could not enter into the joy he felt because she had no fellowship with God. Perhaps she had never been one with her husband in knowing the Lord; maybe she had only been a nominal believer. All the while her husband's faith did not intervene between them she was happy. She did not mind David having his religion so long as it did not affect her life. She was content to go and worship with her husband so long as she was not required to make any changes in her life-style. Like her father Saul she had long neglected the ark of the Lord. She was at ease with her husband's God all the while she could keep her own little idols near at hand.

As she looked at the procession she only saw four men carrying a box on two poles. She only saw the external things. It was just one more religious procession to her and she had certainly seen many of them in the past. Sadly her eyesight was defective. She never realized that the ark symbolized God's presence in the midst of his people, as a foreshadowing of the Lord Jesus Christ in the midst of his church.

WHY DID MICHAL DESPISE DAVID?

She despised David because he was making an exhibition of himself. He was so excited that he had thrown aside all inhibitions as he was taken up with the adoration of his Lord. He wanted to express his deep love and devotion to his God in a way which came naturally to him. Also he had taken off his royal robes because he did not want people to treat him differently from themselves just because he was the king. His desire was to be recognized as a man. He knew that when we come to the end of our lives we all face the same end, whether we are kings or paupers. We must all stand before the judgement seat of Christ (Romans 14:10).

When David finally arrived home his wife was very sarcastic to him. She said, 'How the king of Israel has distinguished himself today, disrobing in the sight of the slave girls of his servants as any vulgar fellow would' (2 Samuel 6:20). But David was not chastened by this outburst; he was learning the secret of humility. He replied, 'I will become even more undignified than this, and I will be humiliated in my own eyes. But by these slave girls you spoke of, I will be held in honour' (6:22).

A truly gracious man does not demand respect from his people; he behaves in such a way that they gladly give it, regardless of how he is dressed. The Lord Jesus never wore any richly embroidered robes, nor sat on any gilded earthly throne. All he was clothed in were simple peasant's robes. The Lord gladly mixed with the common people. Many despised and rejected him (Isaiah 53:3), but those who had eyes to see saw him as 'the Lamb of God who takes away the sin of the world' (John 1:29).

Michal despised David because she misunderstood his motives. She wanted him to be dignified at all times; otherwise it might reflect badly on her. She wanted people to say of her, 'She is the wife, the first and most important wife, of the king.' She never tried to appreciate why David was so excited. The glory of God meant little to her. Her father had neglected the worship of God, and she likewise had little sense of the importance and value of heavenly things.

WHAT HONOUR DID SHE HAVE FROM BEING MARRIED TO THE KING?
She gained nothing of lasting value. She is not even called David's wife in these verses but three times she is referred to as 'the daughter of Saul'. She obviously had high hopes that she would be able to continue Saul's earthly line, but the Lord had rejected Saul. David reminded Michal of this fact when she complained about his behaviour. He said, 'The LORD ... chose me rather than your father or any from his house when he appointed me ruler over the LORD's people Israel' (6:21). That is the reason he wanted to celebrate before the Lord. Despite Michal's opposition he was determined to set right standards of godliness in his own household.

Michal despised David and the Lord and her punishment was to remain childless. She would not carry on her father's line. Saul had rejected the Lord, and she sided with him rather than with her godly husband.

SOME LESSONS FOR US
We must be careful that we do not despise the Lord. We can do this when we despise the laws of God. The Bible should be our guide in everything. If we only read it in the light of modern thinking, then we could be despising the God who wrote it. A little later in this book we will be looking at the appalling story of David's stealing Bathsheba and taking her to be his wife. Nathan the prophet goes to the root of the sin by asking David, 'Why did you despise the word of the LORD by doing what is evil in his sight?' (2 Samuel 12:9).

We despise the Lord when we despise his church. When the Corinthians were behaving in a disorderly way at the Lord's Supper, Paul said, 'Do you despise the church of God?'

(1 Corinthians 11:22). We despise the church when we refuse to accept the teaching of its God-ordained leaders. Amos told the people that they 'hate the one who reproves [them] in court and despise him who tells the truth' (Amos 5:10). Peter also castigates those who 'despise authority' (2 Peter 2:10).

Rather than despising the Lord, we should humbly follow his way. Right at the end of the book of Job we see him standing humbly before the Lord. He says of the Lord that '[you] can do all things; no plan of yours can be thwarted' (Job 42:2). Then he says, 'My ears had heard of you but now my eyes have seen you. Therefore I despise myself and repent in dust and ashes' (Job 42:6).

In humility we should accept that the Lord sends into our lives, even trouble. We should remember the teaching of Proverbs 3:11; 'My son, do not despise the LORD's discipline and do not resent his rebuke, because the LORD disciplines those he loves, as a father the son he delights in.'

FOR FURTHER STUDY

1. Read Matthew 18:20 and meditate on what it means for Christ himself to be present with his people, particularly when they gather together in fellowship (see also Matthew 28:16–20; Haggai 1:13; Acts 18:10).
2. Is it right to give the Mayor or our Member of Parliament a front seat when they join us for a special, maybe civic, service, while others have to sit at the back? (See James 2:1–7; Acts 10:34; Deuteronomy 1:17; Proverbs 23:24).
3. The Bible teaches that the husband is the head of his wife (and his household). What responsibilities does the husband have in regard to

his wife and his household and how can he learn from the example of the Lord Jesus Christ? (see Ephesians 5:25, 28, 33; Colossians 3:19).
4. *How should wives behave with regard to their husbands? (See Ephesians 5:22; Genesis 3:16b; 1 Peter 3:1, 5–6).*
5. *Study the following passages and note the different rôles of men and women: Genesis 2:15–25; Titus 2:1–8; 1 Timothy 2:9–15; 1 Peter 5:1–7.*

TO THINK ABOUT AND DISCUSS

1. *How would you help someone to try to understand the spiritual meaning of religious ritual e.g. the taking of bread and wine at a communion service?*
2. *The Pharisees loved 'to be greeted in the market-places and to have men call them "Rabbi"' (Matthew 23:7). How can we distinguish between being caught up, spiritually, with the joy of our Lord and a desire to be noticed by others for our 'spirituality'?*

5 When God says 'No'

2 Samuel 7:1–16

Are you the kind of person who gets very excited about your good ideas? You think a great deal about them and plan all the details and then you commit the whole thing to God in prayer. You become very excited about a new project which, you believe, will transform your life or the life of the church; and then, after you have presented the fruit of your thinking to the person or group the Lord says, 'No, you can't do it.' Naturally you feel absolutely deflated when this happens. You had placed so much hope in your scheme and truly believed that it would meet many of the needs of the people and answer lots of their questions, but the whole comes to nothing. In such circumstances it is hard not to feel bitter.

This is the kind of situation in which David found himself. He had been a great general of the army, he had captured the stronghold of Zion (i.e. Jerusalem), he had beaten the Philistines in battle and then he had this brilliant idea, 'Let me build a house (a temple) for the ark of God to rest in,' but when he sought God's will in the matter, the prophet told him that God had rejected his plan.

DAVID WAS ENJOYING A TIME OF REST (7:1)

He had certainly earned it. He had expended a great deal of energy while fighting the Philistines and evading capture (and murder) at the hands of King Saul and now, fifteen years later, he was in the position where he could move into the new capital city and enjoy a good period of rest. Perhaps, like us, David discovered that it takes more than just moving all our possessions into our new house to make a home. Much time, planning and effort are needed before a house turns into a home.

What do we do when we have a period of rest and relaxation? Do we venture into this new area with great excitement, forgetting that the Lord is watching everything we do and say? When we go away on holiday do we indulge in the kinds of things that we would never even consider at home, knowing that none of our Christian friends are there to watch us? And do we not bother to go to church when we are away on holiday because none of our friends are there to remind us about worshipping God with his people?

David was not like that. He did not become careless about spiritual matters; in fact he showed a strong desire to serve the Lord. As he looked around his palace he took note of the beautiful home that he had. I am sure he remembered with gratitude Hiram, king of Tyre, who had provided all the expensive materials which had gone into his palace, and as he thought about these things he felt guilty. He was chastened because he realized that he was enjoying a beautiful house, while the ark of God only had a tent to rest in (7:2). It suddenly came over him that this was dishonouring the Lord.

Some centuries later, after the temple had been destroyed by the Chaldeans, Haggai the prophet of the Lord said to the people, 'Is it a time for you yourselves to be living in your panelled houses, while this house (the temple) remains a ruin?' (Haggai 1:4).

It is a disgrace if we, as Christians, are enjoying luxurious living while there are many people who have little to eat, drink or wear are living out in the open all night. It is even more despicable, if we, who claim to be God's people, spend our time, money and talents on our own pleasures, rather than in giving honour and showing respect to our God.

David was an honest man, and he felt so guilty that he went to Nathan the prophet. He had no Bible to refer to in those days and it would be many centuries before that sacred book would be completed. This is the reason God provided prophets who were in close touch with the Lord. These people passed on the message of God to his people.

When David spoke to Nathan, he made a statement which implied a question. He was indirectly asking if he should build a house for the ark, and Nathan's reply was 'go ahead' (7:3). Sometimes we discover God's will by actually doing something rather than just brooding on it. However, rather than rushing into things we should spend more time being still and quiet before the Lord. Whether to move or wait for God to lead us a matter which we should spend long in prayer about.

DAVID RECEIVED A FULLER ANSWER

That same night God spoke to Nathan and the message for David was, 'You are not the one to build me a house' (1 Chronicles 17:4). The Lord was not saying that his concern to build a temple was a bad idea. He was just saying, 'You are not the one to build it.' Many years later David said to his son Solomon, 'My son, I had it in my heart to build a house for the Name of the LORD my God. But this word of the LORD came to me: "You have shed much blood and have fought many wars. You are not to build a home for my Name, because you have shed much blood on the earth in my sight. But you will have a son who will be a man of peace and rest ... He is the one who will build a house for my Name' (1 Chronicles 22:7–10).

It would have been natural for David to be cross at God's rejection but he seems to have accepted it. Then David was given a message of great comfort and strength, 'I took you from the pasture and from following the flock to be ruler over my people Israel. I have been with you wherever you have gone, and I have cut off all your enemies from before you. Now I will make your name great, like the names of the greatest men of the earth' (2 Samuel 7:8–9). The Lord reminded David of the things which he had done for him.

When we are feeling bruised, neglected or ignored because matters have not come up to our expectations, or we have become upset because our ideas have been rejected as unworkable, the Lord often reminds us to look back and remember all the wonderful ways that the Lord has led us.

God proceeded to tell David what he had in store for him. Just because he had said, 'No' to his concern to build a temple that did not mean that God would cast him away. The case was quite the reverse. Through the prophet God told David, 'I will provide a place for my people Israel and will plant them so that they can have a home of their own and no longer be disturbed. Wicked people shall not oppress them any more, as they did at the beginning and have done ever since the time I appointed leaders over my people Israel. I will also give you rest from all your enemies' (7:10–11).

Finally, God took up the theme which was close to David's heart. He said, 'You wanted to build me a house' and the reason I have said, 'No' is because 'I want to build a house for *you*, David' (7:11b). David was not allowed to build a temple for God because the Lord had a much greater rôle for him. He wanted to establish David's house, a new dynasty for him. Saul's line came to an end. Michal never had any children, but David's line was going to be extensive and great. When Saul died, David's son would reign in his place and the Lord told him, 'When your days are over and you rest with your fathers, I will raise up your offspring to succeed you, who will come from your own body, and I will establish his kingdom. He is the one who will build a house for my Name' (7:12–13a).

Many years later Solomon built a temple that was very great and magnificent but later, in the days of Nebuchadnezzar, it would be destroyed. Even the second temple, which King Herod would improve, would be destroyed by Titus in AD 70. All that remains today is a wall which originally was part of its foundations (the Western, or Wailing Wall). However, the house of David (the kingdom of David's line) was going to last for ever. God told David, 'Your house and your kingdom shall endure for ever before me; your throne shall be established for ever' (7:16). The reason for this is because Jesus was born from David's line and he is 'great David's greater Son'. And he will reign for ever and ever (Revelation 11:15).

SOME LESSONS FOR US
How do we react when God says, 'No' to us? Do we accept his

word, or rebel against it and do our own thing? When God says, 'No' to us it almost always means that he has something better for us. We should never be bitter when we see someone else being raised up to do what was in our heart to do.

God is calling us all to be humble and to search our hearts. He wants to encourage us to open up our innermost thoughts and desires to his scrutiny. Our prayer should be, 'Search me, O God, and know my heart: test me and know my anxious thoughts. See if there is any offensive way in me, and lead me in the way everlasting' (Psalm 139:23–24).

FOR FURTHER STUDY

1. Study the following Scriptures and note the importance of periods of rest from our normal work (see Psalm 37:7; Isaiah 40:31; Matthew 11:28–30).
2. Should we still keep the Sabbath as a day of rest? (see Exodus 20:8; Isaiah 56:1–2; Mark 2:27; Hebrews 4:1–5).

TO THINK ABOUT AND DISCUSS

1. Discuss the phrase, 'I'd rather wear out than rust out.' When is it permissible for Christians to take a break from their normal Christian work?
2. Think of an occasion when you believed the Lord was calling you to a specific task (e.g. to be a missionary in some difficult geographical area) yet he made it clear that such a thing was not for you to do. How did you react to his refusal to use you in that way, and what work did he call you to do instead?

6 How to pray

2 Samuel 7:18–29

What do you find the most difficult thing to do as a Christian? Is it going up to a complete stranger in the street and witnessing to them about the Lord Jesus Christ? Is it sitting down with your Bible and puzzling over a complicated passage in one of the prophets, or is it standing up in front of a large crowd of people telling them how you became a Christian?

However hard these things might seem for the average Christian, I think that most of us do not find it easy to come before the Lord and pray. Yet prayer is one of the most wonderful experiences that a Christian can have. In prayer we come face to face with God. We are alone with him and enter right into his presence. We pray when things go wrong in our lives and we are at our wits' end. Prayer is one of the things we do when, for example, we cannot find a drawing pin we have dropped on the floor, or we have mislaid an important document.

In the normal course of our lives prayer is something which does not come easily. We sit, or kneel down, and we start to pray and then our minds wander and we remember things we ought to have done. How sad it is that prayer so often seems to be a chore for us and we are ashamed to admit it.

In the previous chapter of this book we have seen how David was disappointed that he was forbidden to build a temple for God's glory, yet in these following verses we read that David prayed. So in this chapter I want us to find out what we can learn about prayer by examining how David prayed. This section is one of the most wonderful prayers in the whole Bible. It is simple and direct, yet very instructive.

DAVID PRAYED WITH HUMILITY (7:18–21)

The king went into the tent which he had built for the ark of the Lord. At the beginning of the chapter we saw him sitting in his lavish royal palace, but now he is seated in a more humble place, a tent, something that he may have been ashamed of. We know that he had felt that God deserved more than a tent for his dwelling-place.

Nevertheless, David went in and sat before the Lord. He was not being disrespectful by sitting. He felt at ease and he needed to talk with his God. His wonderful plan to build a great temple had been rejected by the Lord, but he had also learned the great news that he was to be the founder of a great dynasty of people. He was so overwhelmed by this news that he wanted to get away from everybody else and be alone with his God.

The sad fact is that many Christians are far too busy in the Lord's work to make the effort to organize their lives so they can spend time alone with God in prayer. He is never too busy to listen to us and speak with us through his word when we spend time praying over it. The Lord Jesus Christ found it very necessary to spend time alone with his Father; so should we.

In his prayer David poured out his heart to God. He asked many questions.

> King David went in and sat before the LORD, and he said: Who am I, O Sovereign LORD, and what is my family, that you have brought me this far? And as if this were not enough in your sight, O Sovereign LORD, you have also spoken about the future of the house of your servant. Is this your usual way of dealing with man, O Sovereign LORD? What more can David say to you? For you know your servant, O Sovereign LORD. For the sake of your word and according to your will, you have done this great thing and made it known to your servant (7:18–21).

It is very noticeable how humble he was. He was the king of Israel who had killed the giant Goliath, led his army in triumph against the Philistines and had gone on to capture the stronghold of the Jebusites, Jerusalem, yet despite all these achievements he gently asked the Lord, 'Who am I, O Sovereign LORD, and what is my family, that you have brought me this far?' He was conscious of God's goodness to him, yet he was very much aware of his own unworthiness. He was not, like the Corinthians, puffed up with a sense of his own importance. He was amazed that God had been so kind to him and honoured him so greatly. It was a further source of amazement to him that God knew him (7:20) and cared about him.

In Psalm 8:4 we read the Psalmist speaking to God, 'What is man that you are mindful of him?' Those of us who lead such busy lives often feel guilty that, in the midst of all our activities, we sometimes forget our wedding anniversary, or it slips our minds to enquire how a sick friend is progressing, but God, who has the whole universe in his care and control, knows each one of us and cares for us. Jesus made this clear when he said, 'Do not worry ... your heavenly Father knows [what you need]' (Matthew 6:32).

David was overwhelmed at God's goodness to him. He said, 'Is this your usual way of dealing with man, O Sovereign LORD?' (7:20). He was amazed that God, who was so great and holy, should bow down and listen to a mere man (even if he were a king). It was almost impossible for him to take it in, yet that is what God has done in Christ Jesus. 'For God so loved the world that he gave his one and only Son, that whoever believes in him shall not perish but have eternal life' (John 3:16). When we think about the incredible grace that there is in the heart of our God then we are brought 'down to size'. Peter tells us, 'Humble yourselves ... under God's mighty hand' (1 Peter 5:6).

If we had just a very small grasp of God's greatness and goodness we would forget our own importance and cast ourselves at his feet and say, 'I'm not worthy of the least of your mercies to me, O Lord.' So if you, just now, are feeling badly treated, if you are puzzled by the way God is leading you, if you are even angry with God, remember that he knows what you are going through and he loves and cares for you.

DAVID PRAYED WITH THANKFULNESS (7:22–24)
He called out, 'How great you are, O Sovereign LORD.' He has a great view of God. He knew that his God was not someone small, puny and insignificant; his God is great, high, holy and lifted up. He is someone who is like no other. Unlike the gods of the heathen David's God was real and the only God who

exists. David never treated the Lord in a light-hearted manner, or as though he were of little account and he gave him the rightful place in his life.

How did David know that God is great? He knew because he had experienced his greatness. He looked back into history and recalled the Lord's dealing with Israel in the past. He redeemed his people Israel. They had been slaves in Egypt for 400 years, but God had planned to rescue them and sent Moses to lead them out of slavery and eventually into the Promised Land.

David recognized that what God did for Israel was unique; he had done nothing like that for any other nation. He says that Israel was 'the one nation that God went out to redeem as a people for himself'. He did not redeem Israel because there was something special about them. It was because he decided to set his love upon them, and save them (see Deuteronomy 7:7).

DAVID PRAYED, RESTING ON GOD'S PROMISE (7:25–29)

David pleaded the promise of God. Long before the time of David God had made a covenant (an agreement) with Israel. He had said that he would be their God and he sealed that promise with the sprinkling of the blood of an animal which had been sacrificed. The people had but to trust him and dedicate their lives in obedience to his law. God said to Israel, 'You will be my people and I will be your God.'

In his prayer David reminded God of that agreement and the promise he had recently given through Nathan that he would raise up one from David's offspring, Solomon, who would build the temple. To see the final fulfillment of God's promise, however, we have to look forward to the coming of the Lord

Jesus Christ, great David's greater Son. Through his birth, life, death on the cross and resurrection, Christ would establish an everlasting kingdom, not of this world (John 18:36), and this promise promise was sealed with the blood of the Lord Jesus which he shed upon the cross of Calvary. That is why the cross is so important.

David reminded God of his promise and then, with great boldness, he said, 'Do as you promised, so that your name will be great for ever' (7:25–26). David knew that God was able to carry out what he had promised. There was no doubt in his mind about the power and ability of the Lord. He was sure that the promise was from God because it had been revealed to him (7:27). He was sure that God's words were trustworthy because he had proved this from his past experience. He knew he could rely on what God had said and was certain that the Lord would never let him down, so he said, 'Now be pleased to bless the house of your servant' (7:29).

We too can plead the promises of God. Jesus, who is God, said, 'Whoever comes to me I will never drive away' (John 6:37). He means that if you call on the name of the Lord, if you go to Jesus in prayer, asking forgiveness through his sacrifice, then he will save you from the consequences of your sin and lead you into his ways.

David rested on the promises of his God and his son was eventually born. Solomon did carry on his line, just as God had promised. We too will discover that if we trust ourselves to him he will carry out all that the Father has promised. We will be new people who respond to his call upon our lives, and we can live in the trustworthiness of God's promise to us that he will be with us, even to the end of the age (Matthew 28:20).

FOR FURTHER STUDY

1. Why is it important under normal circumstances to be on our own when we pray? (See 1 Kings 17:19–20; 2 Kings 4:33; Daniel 6:10; Matthew 5:5–6).

2. What should our attitude be as we pray? (See 2 Chronicles 7:14; Psalm 17:1; 1 Timothy 2:8; Hebrews 10:22).

TO THINK ABOUT AND DISCUSS

1. Share with others some of the difficulties that you experience when you try to set time aside to be alone with the Lord.

2. Discuss why prayer, which should be a wonderful experience for believers, is often the hardest part of the Christian life.

3. Study some of the great hymns on prayer, such as William Cowper's 'What various hindrances we meet in coming to the mercy-seat' or James Montgomery's 'Prayer is the soul's sincere desire, uttered or unexpressed' or John Newton's 'Come, my soul, thy suit prepare, Jesus loves to answer prayer.'

4. Think about Paul's great doxology of praise to God in Romans 11:33–36 and meditate on the wonder of his grace to undeserving sinful people like us.

7 God's free grace

2 Samuel 9:1–13

When I was a young teenager there was a married couple in our church who were very kind to me. They were not very well off and they lived in a small rented house. The husband had a very poorly paid job and their possessions were very few. Although they had a radio, they had no television or car but they were very generous to several of us youngsters. Every Sunday they invited us to tea and sometimes we also went back to their home after the evening service.

I enjoyed those Sundays yet there was one thing that worried me; how was I ever going to be able to repay them for their kindness? The answer came one Sunday evening as we were listening to what was then called the BBC Home Service. Charles Maxwell, a former war correspondent, was telling his audience abut his experiences during the recent war. He spoke about a time when he came across a group of solders who offered him a cup of tea and some food out of their own meagre rations. As he left them he said, 'It's unlikely that we shall ever meet again so how can I repay you for your kindness?' One of the solders merely said, 'Pass it on, mate.' Then Maxwell quoted a very old hymn from the Moody and Sankey collection,

FACE2FACE: **DAVID**

> Have you had a kindness shown?
> Pass it on!
> 'Twas not given for thee alone;
> Pass it on!
> Let it travel down the years,
> Let it wipe another's tears,
> Till in heaven the deed appears—
> Pass it on![1]

During the fifty years and more since that time many people have also shown great kindness to me, but I have never forgotten that broadcast and I have tried to pass on to others the kindness which has been shown to me.

As we look at 2 Samuel 9 we notice that David is sitting comfortably in his palace at Jerusalem and is looking back over his past life and contemplating all the good things that others have done for him. He remembers the happy times of fellowship he had with Jonathan, the king's son; and he is sad as he recalls that both Jonathan and his father Saul are dead, as well as many other sons of the late king.

As David mulls over these things in his mind, perhaps these words of Jonathan came back to him, 'Show me unfailing kindness like that of the LORD as long as I live, … and do not ever cut off your kindness from my family' (1 Samuel 20:14–15). It seems then that David was moved as he thought again of those promises and that covenant which he and Jonathan had made with each other.

DAVID'S KINDNESS TO MEPHIBOSHETH

As David dwelt on these things he asked his servants, 'Is there anyone still left of the house of Saul to whom I can show kindness for Jonathan's sake?' (9:1). David wanted to find out if there were any survivors of Saul's line so he could show kindness to them. He had promised Jonathan that he would do so and he wanted to keep his word.

Keeping our promises is a very important thing to do, and we are very poor Christians if we fail to do so. How often do we attend meetings where missionaries are speaking and we tell them that we will continue to pray for them when they return to the mission field? We take their prayer letters and we seek God's blessing on them and their work, but after a while we get slack and eventually we often forget them altogether. Our God is not like that. He promised that 'as long as the earth endures, seedtime and harvest, cold and heat, summer and winter, day and night will never cease' (Genesis 8:23). He also made this promise to his people, 'I will never leave you nor forsake you' (Hebrews 13:5). It is a blessing that God never forgets to keep his promises to his people.

David's overwhelming burden was to show kindness to any survivor of Saul's household 'for Jonathan's sake'. He felt a warm glow every time he thought about his friend. The love that he and Jonathan had for each other was rich, honest and true, and he wanted to do a kindness to someone in memory of his friend. His enquiries eventually led to a surviving servant of Saul called Ziba. From him he learned the news that one of Jonathan's sons was still alive. His name was Mephibosheth, but he was lame in both of his feet. It would seem that Ziba was implying that because he was a cripple David would think that it was not worth spending much effort on him. 2 Samuel 4:4 tells us how he became like this. After Saul had died there was much in-fighting and intrigue as various descendants of the king tried to gain the rule over Israel. During one of these uprisings the nurse who looked after five-year old Mephibosheth took him in her arms and fled with him. Unfortunately in the confusion the little lad seems to have fallen from the nurse's arms and hurt himself. The result was that for the rest of his life he was crippled in both of his feet.

However, David was not deterred by this news. He immediately asked Ziba, 'Where is he?' and he was told, 'He is at the house of Makir son of Ammiel in Lo Debar' (9:4). This is all we are told about the early years of Mephibosheth except that by this time he was old enough to have a young son of his own (9:12) so he must have been at least in his late teens. We do not know much about Lo Debar either, but seems that Mephibosheth was living a fairly quiet, if harsh, life away from all of the activity of any large township.

I wonder what Mephibosheth was thinking as he was brought to David's capital. He must have wondered if he were going to be put to death; this often happened when a new dynasty came into power in ancient times to ensure that there was no one left to claim the throne on behalf of the earlier ruler.

It is not surprising then that as Mephibosheth came to David he 'bowed down to pay him honour' (9:6). His heart must have been beating very fast as he prostrated himself before the king. We can almost sense the stillness as this young man made obeisance to David. The silence was eventually broken by the king. He spoke just one word, 'Mephibosheth!' 'Your servant,' the cripple replied but instead of being vindictive, David spoke kindly to him and said, 'Don't be afraid ... for I will surely show you kindness for the sake of your father Jonathan.' Then the king gave orders that the land which had belonged to Mephibosheth's grandfather Saul be given to him. Instead of living in a place where there was no or little pasture, Mephibosheth was told that he would always be welcomed to eat at the king's table, even though he considered himself unworthy of such an honour.

What a lovely story this is of generous and gracious kindness being shown to an undeserving cripple, one who could never repay David. Even more surprising is that this happened 3,000 years ago, before equal opportunity laws were put on the statute books of civilized countries.

GOD'S KINDNESS TO UNDESERVING SINNERS

Every born-again Christian bears a remarkable similarity to Mephibosheth. We have all been crippled by a fall, but the fall that incapacitated us was the one that Adam our forefather had. Before we were saved we had no appetite for Bible study or sermons or prayer. Before we knew Christ's salvation we had no taste for such things. In our former life we had nothing to commend us to God. We were just as worthless as crippled Mephibosheth felt himself to be. In our sin and selfishness what use were we to God? We were far off and we had no rights or anything at all which could commend us or enable us to approach the Lord's royal presence. But then God moved into the situation and he called us to come to him, just as David fetched Mephibosheth (he couldn't walk on his own). If we think about our state before we came to Christ then we will acknowledge that there was nothing in us that would be attractive to our Lord. We belonged to another kingdom (not Saul's, but Satan's). However, God so loved us that he stooped down and lifted us up out of the slimy pit and out of the mud and mire and set our feet on a rock (see Psalm 40:2). Before we were converted we had no desire or ability to approach King Jesus. Isaiah describes the world without Christ like this, 'All of us have become like one who is unclean, and all our righteous acts are like filthy rags; we all shrivel up like a leaf, and like the wind our sins sweep us away. No-one calls on your name or strives to lay hold of you; for you have hidden your face from us and made us waste away because of our sins' (Isaiah 64:6–7). It was just as if we were far off from God and there seemed no way for us to approach him. Again Isaiah puts it so vividly, 'From the sole of your foot to the top of your head there is no soundness—only wounds and bruises and open sores, not cleansed or bandaged or soothed with oil' (Isaiah 1:6).

Just as David took the initiative, so did God. He sent his Son, the Lord Jesus Christ, into this poor sin-sick world and he opened up a way for us to approach God. He did this by sending Jesus to that cruel cross so that he could offer his pure sinless body as a sacrifice for us. Jesus' death paid the price of our sin. The shedding of his precious blood cleansed us and made it possible for us to be born again and brought into God's kingdom.

Our salvation came about because we repented of our sin and turned to God through faith in the Lord Jesus Christ, but how did it happen that we wanted to turn to Christ? Isaac Watts expresses it like this,

Why was I made to hear his voice,

And enter while there's room;

While thousands make a wretched choice,

And rather starve than come?

Just as Mephibosheth fell at the feet of David, so we cast ourselves on Christ's mercy when we came and sought his salvation. We knew that we were sinners and we could not understand why Christ should care about us. Paul behaved similarly on the Damascus road. 'As he neared Damascus ..., suddenly a light from heaven flashed around him. He fell to the ground and heard a voice say to him, "Saul, Saul, why do you persecute me?"' (Acts 9:4). Like Mephibosheth and Paul we waited in awe before the Lord, to hear his verdict on our sinfulness, until the silence was broken by Jesus Christ himself. Just as he gently said, 'Mary' to the visitor in the garden of Gethsemane, so he called each of his own blood-bought people by their names. He knows each one of us and graciously says, 'Son, daughter, your sins which are many are all forgiven you. Don't be afraid, I am with you and will bless you' (see Luke 7:47–48; Isaiah 41:10).

The wonderful news is that we no longer have to live in the darkness of this world, where there is little to satisfy us. Jesus calls us to eat at his own table. When we were born again we became members of his family. We live continually in his presence and we can say of the Lord Jesus Christ, 'Like an apple tree among the trees of the forest is my lover among the young men. I delight to sit in his shade, and his fruit is sweet to my taste. He has taken me to the banquet hall, and his banner over me is love' (Song 2:3–4).

Like Mephibosheth we step back in wonder and readily admit that we do not deserve such blessings.

FOR FURTHER STUDY

1. *List some of the precious promises in God's word (see Acts 13:32; Romans 9:4; Galatians 3:16; 2 Peter 1:3–4).*

2. David's kindness to Mephibosheth is a pale shadow of the kindness that God shows us in granting us the blessings of his grace. What are some of these spiritual blessings that are given to believers? (See Romans 2:4; Ephesians 2:7; Titus 3:4).

TO THINK ABOUT AND DISCUSS

1. Share some of the promises that you have failed to keep (e.g. to pray regularly for certain missionaries). Discuss what you can do to rectify the situation.

2. Discuss how you can share with others some of the undeserved blessings you have received from the Lord.

3. Are there any promises that God makes in the Bible that you find difficult to accept or understand?

Notes

1 **Henry Burton,** No. 802 in *Sacred Songs and Solos, revised and enlarged* (London: Morgan and Scott, c. 1875).

8 David's foolish night

2 Samuel 11:1–5

It is frightening to count up how many times we sin each day. If we were to multiply these we could find out how many sins we commit in a whole year. So it would be horrifying to realize what sins we have committed and are likely to be guilty of during our whole lifetime. We who really want to live holy lives are easily attracted to the 'delights' of sin that are emblazoned all around us, in advertising hoardings, magazines, newspapers and on the television.

King David never had these things to tempt him but he certainly succumbed to the lusts of the flesh (1 John 2:16) and he paid the price for his sinful behaviour. This is probably the most well-known story about David apart from the fight between David and Goliath. It is amazing that King David, the Old Testament saint who wrote so many lovely psalms, sinned grievously.

In 2 Samuel 11 we have this story of lust, adultery, intrigue, deceit and murder. It is no surprise that Hollywood has made it into numerous films and many stage plays and operas have been based upon it.

FACE2FACE: **DAVID**

DAVID'S PLEASURE

The story starts in the springtime (11:1). There is a well-known saying that in the spring a young man's fancy turns to love, but David was no young man by this stage of his life. He was about 50 years old. He had worked very hard all his life and he had fought hard too. In chapter 10:17 we see that David was still leading his army against his enemies. During the previous twenty years since he had set up his capital in Jerusalem he had done much to extend the borders of his kingdom. Because the nation of Israel was now established as a powerful force, David could justifiably be proud of his achievements.

As this chapter starts we see the king waving off his army as they went out to fight once again. The winter was over, the crops had been gathered in, the weather had improved and the season of fighting had begun once again. Only this time 'when kings go off to war' David did not. Perhaps he was feeling too old. Certainly no one could accuse him of not doing his bit and in any case he had a good general, Joab, to lead the army. Joab had proved his good fighting qualities. He was a ruthless man who obeyed the king's command to the letter. Yet he could use his initiative as well. David could certainly stay at home, resting content knowing that Joab would not let him down.

His general certainly had some great officers with him. These men were legendary in Israel and everyone knew about their courageous exploits. They were called 'David's mighty men'. In fact, nearly a whole chapter is devoted to them (2 Samuel 23). Among their number was Asahel the brother of Joab. Then there were Abi-Albon the Arbathite and Eliam son of Ahithophel the Gilonite and right at the end of the list we read about a man called 'Uriah the Hittite'. It is he who becomes one of the four main characters in this story.

Despite all of these strong men, the question still remains, 'Why did David stay at home?' Certainly if he had gone to war, as he had always done in the past, then perhaps he would not have fallen into temptation. As it happened the whole of David's subsequent life was coloured by that decision to remain in Jerusalem.

It is amazing how our lives can be completely transformed by one little act—even when we choose to do nothing. I am forcibly reminded about that fact when I am driving on a motorway and I come across a very nasty crash that had probably only taken place a few minutes before. I realize then that if I had not had been held up at traffic lights earlier (a delay which I had been cross about) I might well be lying dead in the rubble of the crash. Sometimes we do not know what we have been preserved from and what might have occurred if we had taken a different course of action. However, we do know this, 'We cannot count upon divine protection when we forsake the path of duty.'[1]

In 2 Samuel 11 we read that David 'had left his armour off', and it seems that he indulged in too much laziness. Verse 2 indicates that he was resting on his bed in the late afternoon. He would never have been able to do that had he been with his army on the battle field. The old saying is true, 'The Devil finds work for idle hands (and minds) to do.' We find that young people quite often get into mischief because they are bored and say they have nothing to do. Certainly we all need to have adequate rest and relaxation but we should never let things slide so much that are 'caught off guard'.

Perhaps David had stayed at home because he had grown too complacent. He wanted an easy life, having worked very hard up until that time. In church life we sometimes hear people say something like, 'I've done my bit; let others do the work now,' but in the kingdom of God there is no excuse for sheer laziness. I knew an old woman in her nineties who was blind and unable to get about, but every Sunday morning and evening and every Wednesday evening she knew who was preaching and leading the Bible study at the church of which I was then the pastor, and she prayed earnestly for them. She had never seen some of the people she prayed for but still laboured on and when she was called to be with her Lord we missed the effects of her prayers. She often encouraged me by saying, 'You always give a call to the unsaved, whenever you are preaching.'

Back in Jerusalem, on that particular late afternoon or early evening, David went for a walk on his roof. There is nothing wrong with that. Roofs were made flat and were especially suitable for an evening stroll. Up there David would have been away from the dust and dirt of the streets and he would have had the cool of the evening breeze wafting around him and the view from that height was especially pleasing and relaxing. He would have been able to look up to the hills and contemplate their strength and security. This would have reminded him that his strength came from the Lord, but there were other things that he could see too.

No doubt his palace was among the highest of all the buildings in Jerusalem. From the roof he could look down and see things which were normally hidden from the streets and the tops of other smaller houses. I imagine he could see an old woman burying rubbish in the ground at the back of her house. Maybe he could see a child hiding another child's toy in a hole near the corner of the wall. And also he could see a woman carrying out her ritual washing, following the end of her menstrual cycle, even though she might well have been hidden from everyone else's eyes. As he looked more intently, he noticed that this particular woman was very beautiful.

Had David gone up on his roof at that particular time because he had glimpsed this woman before and he hoped that she would show herself again? If so I wonder whether he would have calculated that she might be having a bath at the time. Certainly when he looked down from his flat roof on that evening he saw this woman bathing. Any gentleman would have looked away as soon as he realized what was happening. He would have got down from the roof immediately for fear of causing her embarrassment, but David was no gentleman. He gazed at the woman and the more he looked, the more he realized that she was very beautiful indeed. Apart from fighting, the one thing that David had a great deal of experience of was beautiful women. Not only did David keep looking, but he sent someone to make enquiries about her. The servant came back with a message which he put in the form of a question, 'Isn't this Bathsheba, the daughter of Eliam and the wife of Uriah the Hittite?' (11:3).

The servant was very wise. Perhaps he used this form of words to warn David that he should be very careful. Was her father the same Eliam who was a member of David's personal bodyguard? Was the servant saying, 'You know that Eliam is very precious to you so be careful that you do not harm his daughter'? Even more important was the statement that she

FACE2FACE: **DAVID**

was the wife of Uriah the Hittite. Uriah was also one of David's trusted loyal soldiers. Most important of all the servant was saying, 'She is a married woman.'

David ought to have stopped there and then. If he were in need of intimate female company then he had plenty of ladies to choose from. He had four wives and a great number of concubines. Surely one of them could have satisfied him so why did his eyes wander to another man's wife? It was because Satan was tempting him to satisfy his lusts even though he knew that he was sinning against the law of God, and against Uriah. Paul was to say, much later, 'Put on the full armour of God so that you can take your stand against the devil's schemes' (Ephesians 6:11). But David had taken his armour off. He was not prepared to do battle with Satan, but he was willing to stifle his conscience and ignore the warnings of his faithful servant.

It appears that straightaway 'David sent messengers to get her'. Notice the brutal language that the sacred writer uses here. The Bible continues, 'She came to him, and he slept with her' (11:4) but what a devastating effect that one moment of intense pleasure brought to David. Afterwards he felt exhilarated and fulfilled. He must have been very pleased with himself but notice the last verse in this chapter, 'The thing David had done displeased the LORD' (11:27).

DAVID'S PROBLEM

Bathsheba went home and her husband was fighting across the Jordan. He would have known nothing about David's actions or his wife's infidelity. Great care would surely have been taken to ensure that the neighbours did not find out what she had done. I am confident that attempts were made to cover up David's immoral fling.

Some time later when possibly David had forgotten about the event he received a message from Bathsheba. All it said was, 'I am pregnant' (11:5). Imagine what would have flashed through David's mind when he received that message. His thoughts would have been in turmoil. Bathsheba's husband had been away for many months, fighting in David's army. If Bathsheba gave birth to a child, Uriah would know that it was not his but Bathsheba would know who the real father was because she had slept with David just after the purification following her menstrual cycle (11:4). Even those little comments give added point to the story. God's word is true, and even the smallest comments must be noted. There is nothing irrelevant or unnecessary in the Bible.

David realized he had to do something about this awful situation. If he were found out, it would be disastrous for him, his kingdom and the cause of God. He could not blame his sin on the lusts of youth; he was fifty years old. He was a married man, and some of his sons were men themselves. He was the king of Israel, God's own precious people. Furthermore, Uriah was away on the king's service, fighting for him. While Bathsheba's husband was away showing his loyalty to the king, David had been disloyal to him and had committed adultery with his wife. Furthermore, David was a child of God and it was his responsibility to lead his people into the ways of God.

What a mess everything was! But that one night of ecstasy was not the whole story. One writer has said, 'The affair with Bathsheba was the climax of twenty years of carelessness with regard to the warning of God concerning kings.'[2] In Deuteronomy 17:16–17 there are three commands which were specifically given to any future king of Israel. The first says, 'The king ... must not acquire great numbers of horses for himself.' David seems to have passed that test. The third command was, 'He must not accumulate large amounts of silver and gold.' David's son Solomon might have become guilty of this but David did not appear to be selfish in this respect. However, the second requirement says, '[The king] must not take many wives, or his heart will be led astray.' Although David's predecessors and many of his successors only had one wife, David disobeyed this clear command and had many wives. Michal, Saul's daughter, was his first wife. Then he married Abigail, the widow of Nabal, then Ahinoam of Jezreel. While living at Hebron, he married four more wives. Then, when he moved his home to Jerusalem, he added even more wives and concubines. Theodore Epp comments, 'These rules for the kings of Israel were given so that they might discipline themselves and be saved from the very thing that caused David's downfall. His sin with Bathsheba was more than the passion of a moment because for twenty years he had been sowing the seeds of fleshly indulgence, and then ended in this terrible iniquity.'[3]

On top of everything else David knew the law of God. This said, 'If a man commits adultery with another man's wife—with the wife of his neighbour—both the adulterer and the adulteress must be put to death' (Leviticus 20:10). This was given to the people by God many years before David's time and God's laws apply to kings as much as they apply to common folk.

OUR PROBLEM

We are all tempted in one way or another. Adulterous relationships are hurled at us every day from our newspapers and television sets. Christians are tempted to think, 'I'm too honourable to commit such a sin,' but if David could have succumbed to such a thing, then so could any of us. Jesus said, 'Anyone who looks at a woman lustfully has already committed adultery with her in his heart' (Matthew 5:28) and it is not only men who are tempted in this way!

Yet sex is not the only thing which can tempt us. Some people are tempted by money and they steal, or hoard up for themselves cash which could be given to help other more needy people. Some are tempted by beautiful possessions and they buy them, not because they need them, but purely to satisfy their lust to own things. And all of us are tempted by selfishness; we want others to think well of us, but James warns us, 'Each one is tempted when, by his own evil desire, he is dragged away and enticed. Then, after desire has conceived, it gives birth to sin: and sin, when it is full-grown, gives birth to death' (James 1:14–15).

How can we avoid temptation? We can be careful where we put our eyes. The psalmist prayed, 'Turn my eyes away from worthless things' (Psalm 119:37). The story of his adultery starts with these words, '[David] saw a woman bathing' (11:3). We should ensure that we do not look at those things which could lead us into temptation. Job made a covenant with his eyes 'not to look lustfully at a girl' (Job 31:1).

We should also be careful where we go. David did not have to go up on his roof (certainly he did not have to go at that particular time). We should avoid those places where we are likely to be tempted to sin so the very best thing that we can do is to turn our eyes away from sin, and look to Jesus.

FOR FURTHER STUDY

1. How can we avoid being tempted to sin? (See Isaiah 52:11–12; 1 Corinthians 6:18–20; 1 Timothy 6:11; 2 Timothy 2:22).
2. What steps did Jesus take to overcome the temptations of the devil? (See Matthew 4:1–11; Mark 1:12–13; Luke 4:1–13).
3. What means does the devil use to lead us into temptation? (See Genesis 3:13; Proverbs 1:10; Matthew 6:13; 2 Corinthians 11:3; 1 Peter 5:8–9).

TO THINK ABOUT AND DISCUSS

1. Discuss an occasion when you were tempted to sin and explain how you intend to avoid being caught up in such a situation again.
2. Explain the steps you would take in helping a young person (or weak Christian) who finds him or herself caught up in sinful behaviour.
3. Discuss this saying, 'It's all right to look, but not touch.'

Notes

1 **A. W. Pink,** *Life of David,* vol. 2, chapter 51, 'His Fearful Fall'.
2 **Theodore H. Epp,** *David* (Back to the Bible, 1965), p. 123.
3 Ibid. p. 123.

9 David's attempted cover-up

2 Samuel 11:6–27

David ought to have known better than to entice a beautiful young woman into his bedroom. In itself it was unwise but even more so because David was a godly king and Bathsheba was already married to one of the most loyal and brave officers in his army. The whole matter was extremely sordid.

In the previous chapter of this book we saw how David had totally disregarded God's laws and indulged in laziness rather than wanting to honour the Lord. When temptation came in the form of his noticing a woman bathing in a house below his rooftop, David failed to avert his eyes. It was that closer look that led him into a catalogue of trouble. Then later on when David learned that Bathsheba was pregnant with his child he panicked. Instead of immediately confessing his sin and doing what he could to make amends, he tried to cover up his wrongdoing and that is always an irresponsible thing to do.

If we ignore the cry of our guilty conscience then we will soon discover that we become more and more estranged from the Lord. We find that we cannot pray as we did formerly, we feel that God is far off from us and we become introspective and believe that no one loves us any more.

James, writing many centuries after David had died, tells us what happens when anyone allows their sin to fester. His words could well be a commentary on this story; perhaps he had David and Bathsheba in mind when he wrote, 'Each one is tempted when, by his own evil desire, he is dragged away and enticed. Then, after desire has conceived, it gives birth to sin; and sin, when it is full-grown, gives birth to death' (James 1:14–15). James emphasizes the thought of 'desire' which he tells us builds up into 'enticing', 'conceiving' and finally 'giving birth' to sin. These phrases illustrate what happened to David and Bathsheba. David's sin gave birth to death, but it was not the death of the king, but that of an innocent man, the husband of Bathsheba, Uriah the Hittite,

DAVID PANICKED (11:6)

It would seem that the first thing David did was to send a message to Joab, who was out on the battlefield. Perhaps the king did this immediately he heard the worrying news that Bathsheba was expecting a child. His main aim was not the welfare of Bathsheba or his child; it seems that all he wanted to do was to clear his name. He had a vital reputation to uphold and his own future was what was uppermost in his mind. He was far more concerned to conceal his crime than to seek God's forgiveness. Proverbs tells us, 'He who conceals his sins does not prosper' but it graciously adds, 'whoever confesses and renounces them finds mercy' (Proverbs 28:13). What did David do in his trouble? He contacted his army general with this message, 'Send me Uriah the Hittite.'

It seems very strange to us that this great man of God, who so often communed with the Lord in prayer, first of all sent to

Joab. Why did he not get down on his knees and seek God's face in prayer before he attempted to defend himself? Sadly we can understand why David acted like this, because we do the same kind of thing when we are in deep trouble. We know that we ought to seek God in prayer because prayer is a wonderful weapon we can wield in our fight against the evil one. It is a blessed comfort too for all those who are in trouble. David knew this, yet he did not avail himself of it.

Perhaps David was really being very honest. He knew that he had sinned and sinned grievously so he could not expect God to act as though everything were all right. When we have sinned we cannot hope that God will immediately come to our aid to sort everything out. First of all we must seek his forgiveness. A.W. Pink said, 'Refusal to put things right with God and our fellow men and women, by confessing our sins, gives Satan a great advantage.'[1] We can be sure that the devil will get in wherever we give him the opportunity and he will spoil our work and witness.

David did none of these things. Instead he sent for Bathsheba's husband, not to ask his forgiveness for the wrong he had done to him but so that he could wriggle out of his predicament. He had a cunning plan up his sleeve, but it would only work if Uriah would co-operate without him without knowing anything about Bathsheba's pregnancy! When Uriah arrived at the palace David set out to humour him. He asked him how the war was going and he gave him the impression that he was an important official whose opinion he valued. We can see how David's scheme was unfolding. He wanted Uriah to relax and be at his ease in the royal presence. After a great deal of flattery David turned to Uriah and said, 'Go home now.'

A TIME OF RELAXATION (11:8–11)

David told Uriah, 'Go down to your house and wash your feet.' In other words, 'Go home and have a good rest—put your feet up' (see Genesis 18:4; 19:2). Of course David wanted Uriah to go home and sleep with his wife so that there would be no hint of scandal when the child was born to Bathsheba. It was a simple plan that should have worked in those days before DNA testing. Robert Burns tells us that the best-laid schemes of mice and men can go wrong, and this one certainly did. Numbers 32:23 tells us, 'You may be sure that your sin will find you out.'

It seems incredible that a soldier should miss out on the opportunity to have a bit of leave. But after he went out of the palace door, Uriah 'slept at the entrance to the palace with all his master's servants and did not go down to his house' (11:9). We do not know whether he suspected something, but instead of going to Bathsheba he stayed with the servants. This fact is stated several times (see verses 8, 9 and 10).

When David was told that Uriah did not go home he was very worried so he asked him, 'Haven't you just come from a distance? Why didn't you go home?'(11:10). Uriah replied, 'The ark and Israel and Judah are staying in tents, and my master Joab and my lord's men are camped in the open field. How could I go to my house to eat and drink and *lie with my wife*? As surely as you live, I will not do such a thing' (italics mine).

Possibly there may have been a slight rebuke in Uriah's words because the king stayed and enjoyed the luxury of the palace while his men were sleeping on the hard ground. Whatever the case, this loyal soldier felt that it would be quite wrong for him to enjoy himself while his companions were out on the battlefield.

When David learned that Uriah had not spent the night with Bathsheba, he must have been in a great quandary. His wonderful plan, which he thought could not fail, did. Just as Pilate had no desire to order the execution of Jesus, neither did David wish to cause the death of his loyal friend. Yet he did not want to be exposed as an adulterer, so he dreamed up one final scheme. He said to himself, 'I'll get him drunk and then he's bound to be so stupefied that he will automatically go home and sleep with his wife.' So, to soften up Uriah, David kept him waiting in Jerusalem for two more days (11:12). It would have been quite natural for Uriah to visit his wife, but he felt that would be disloyal to his fellow-soldiers. It is a pity that David had not exercised the same kind of determination to do the right thing when he saw Bathsheba bathing.

Eventually David sent for Uriah and sat him down to a large feast with so much wine that Uriah became drunk. The Bible does not condemn the use of alcohol but it most certainly warns us against drunkenness. It is a shameful thing for any believer to get into such a state that he is not in full charge of his senses. Proverbs 23:31–32 tells us, 'Do not gaze at wine when it is red, when it sparkles in the cup, when it goes down smoothly! In the end it bites like a snake and poisons like a viper.'

At the end of the meal David must have thought to himself, 'Now he's drunk, he'll forget about his vow to stay here and all he will think about is going home to the arms of his beautiful wife.' However verse 13b tells us, 'In the evening Uriah went out to sleep on his mat among his master's servants' and it adds, very pointedly, 'he did not go home.'

When David heard this news he was absolutely furious; he had come to end of his tether. Uriah had failed to take the easy and pleasant way out; now he would have to pay for it the hard way. David did not want to murder Uriah but what else could he do? He had his reputation to think of! The action which he next took was the cause of a huge blot on David's character, a stain which remained with him for the rest of his life. After he was dead this sin would still be remembered.

In 1 Kings 15:5 we read about Abijah, a descendant of David. There the Lord commends David and says, 'David had done what was right in the eyes of the LORD and had not failed to keep any of the LORD's commands all the days of his life—except in the case of Uriah the Hittite.'

DAVID SENT A LETTER (11:12–15)
In the morning, when David's head was clear and he knew what he was going to do, he wrote a letter to Joab, his field commander. 'Put Uriah in the front line where the fighting is fiercest. Then withdraw from him so that he will be struck down and die.' What a death sentence that was. Was this how battles ought to be fought? Surely any soldier fighting in such a precarious position should be supported, not left to take the brunt of any counter-attack! But that is what David ordered, and that is how Joab carried out the plan. It is even more ironical to realize that Uriah was the one who carried this letter back to the battlefield and handed it over to Joab.

How cruel of David to do this. Not only did he order his certain death but he devised a scheme whereby it would seem that he would be killed in battle—and Uriah himself was instructed to carry his own death warrant to the place of his execution. So finally David achieved his end. The battle was so waged that Uriah and many other valiant men all died. But it was all so unnecessary. Any other commander would have failed to send his men so close to the wall. The Israelites would have learned the folly of that way of attack back in the time of the Judges when Abimelech was killed by a woman throwing a millstone on him from the wall so that he died in Thebez (Judges 9:50–54).

Eventually, when David was told the news about how many of his mighty men had fallen in battle, instead of being angry with Joab's bad conduct of the battle, all he said in effect was, 'Never mind, these things happen' (11:25). However, there is one phrase which pounds through these last verses in chapter 11. Its ominous tones jar us like the opening first four repeated notes of Beethoven's Fifth Symphony—'Uriah is dead.' 'Uriah is dead' (11:21 and 24). None of the other dead are named, only Uriah. That, of course, is what David wanted to know. He must have thought to himself, 'Now that Uriah is no more, the heat will be turned away from me and everything will be all right once more.'

Eventually, after a respectable space for mourning, Bathsheba became David's wife and she bore him a son, but that is not the end of the story. David and Bathsheba did not live happily ever after; nor did the baby. They would certainly have had carnal pleasure in each other's arms but the chapter ends with these ominous words, 'But the thing David had done displeased the LORD' (11:27).

No-one, even the king, can escape from displeasing the Lord. That is a very serious matter. Before David's relationship with God was restored, he had to be brought

FACE2FACE: **DAVID**

down very, very low in humble confession of his sin. Psalm 51 is David's confession of his sin with regard to Bathsheba. The Lord certainly forgives those who humbly repent of their sin and return to faith in God, but that did not mean that David did not have to suffer for his actions. Even though his fellow-citizens may never have found out about his adultery, God knew about it and he was displeased.

FOR FURTHER STUDY
1. What part does conscience play in our Christian life? (See 1 Corinthians 8:7–13; 1 Timothy 1:5, 19; 2 Timothy 1:3; Hebrews 10:22; 1 Peter 3:16).
2. See what you can learn about obedience to God by examining some of the people in the Bible who put duty to God and their fellow-men before their own comfort (see Genesis 12:1–4; 1 Kings 17:5; Acts 26:19–23; Hebrews 12:2).
3. What does the Bible say about the use of alcohol? (See Isaiah 5:11; Proverbs 20:1; Luke 21:34; Ephesians 5:18).

TO THINK ABOUT AND DISCUSS

1. Tell how you, or someone you have heard about, tried to cover up wrong-doing. What did you, or they, learn about life, and specifically the Christian life, from following this foolish path?
2. Are there things that you have done, perhaps in order to save your reputation, and of which you are now ashamed? What steps can be taken to try to put matters right with God and those who were involved and perhaps still are implicated by these acts?
3. Study Psalms 32 and 51 and think about the need for a sincere confession of sin before experiencing the joy of forgiveness.

Notes

1 **A. W. Pink,** *Life of David*, vol. 2, Chapter 52, 'His Terrible Sin' on http://www.pbministries.org/books/pink/David/Vol2/david2_52.htm.

10 David's sin uncovered

2 Samuel 12:1–12

How foolish it is to try to cover up our sin. The Bible makes it very clear that we have all sinned and even the best among us are prone to think or do things that are wrong (Romans 3:23). As we have seen in the previous chapter of this book, David's sin was great and he tried to remove any trace of it.

It is very uncomfortable for any leader to be approached by a member of his church or group and have his faults pointed out to him. In 2 Samuel 12 it is not just any leader who is reproved but the king of Israel, and the one doing the challenging is Nathan the prophet of the Lord.

A GODLY MESSENGER

Around nine months had passed and it seemed that David had got away with his adultery and the murder of Uriah. He had been dead for some while and the way had been opened up for David to marry his widow. We do not know whether the people suspected that David was the father of the expected child but it is recorded that, 'the thing David had done displeased the LORD' (11:27).

Whenever we disobey any of God's laws we displease him.

Yet the amazing thing is that our God is not vindictive. He is certainly hurt by our sinfulness and he makes sure that we do not escape punishment even though nine months (or nine years) may have gone past without anything untoward happening to us. Eventually God's law will be upheld and we are 'brought to book'. However, the Lord is gracious and, by his Spirit working in our consciences, he calls us to repent of our sin. Not only that, he forgives us if we are truly penitent and then he sends us on our way with the ability to hold up our head once again.

In David's case the Lord sent his prophet Nathan to the king (12:11). Nathan must have been aware of what had been going on. He was the Lord's servant and would very likely have had special insight into the affair of David and Bathsheba. But he knew also that as the Lord's prophet he had the responsibility to do something about sin, even when it was the king who had done the sinning! So eventually at the Lord's leading he went up to the royal palace. We are not told that David sent for him. This is not surprising because when a person is out of fellowship with God because of sin, the last person they want around them is a godly prophet. Certainly, just when he was feeling that everything was now going well with him, the king did not want to be made to feel uncomfortable.

I wonder if Nathan trembled, knowing that it was his duty to confront the king with his sinfulness. It is always difficult to approach a friend and tell them something which we know they will not want to hear. The old question arises when there is a problem, 'Should I tell my best friend?'

First of all, he made sure of his facts. So often rumours blow things up out of all proportion; we cannot merely act on hearsay or suspicion. Secondly, Nathan chose the right time to speak to the king and thirdly, he weighed up his words carefully and spoke wisely to his sovereign. Proverbs 25:11 tells us, 'A word aptly spoken is like apples of gold in settings of silver'.

Nathan did not speak out of selfishness, nor did he speak in haste. He made certain of his facts and he used diplomatic language. He was, after all, addressing his king. Paul gives us good advice and a warning in Galatians 6:1, 'Brothers, if someone is caught in a sin, you who are spiritual should restore him gently. But watch yourself, or you also may be tempted.' If we take any other approach, it can easily lead to a misunderstanding, or maybe disaster.

A GODLY MESSAGE

This is the way Nathan went about his difficult task. He told David a story about a rich man who had a traveller visit him. He had to give him something to eat but instead of taking one of the many sheep and cattle he owned to prepare a meal, he took the only, and much loved, lamb of his poor neighbour, and he killed that animal so that his visitor could have a meal.

This was not only an interesting story but a believable one too. David appears to think that Nathan was speaking about an actual incident that had taken place in his kingdom because we read that 'David burned with anger against the [rich] man and said to Nathan, "As surely as the LORD lives, the man who did this deserves to die! He must pay for that lamb four times over, because he did such a thing and had no pity"' (12:5–6). David actually referred to the law of the Lord because Exodus

22:1 says, 'If a man steals ... a sheep and slaughters it ... he must pay back ... four sheep for the sheep.' The law did not say that the man should be put to death but David added that because he was so incensed about the situation.

Nathan waited patiently for David to finish his outburst of righteous indignation, then he spoke four simple words—probably the most terrifying words that David was ever to hear—'You are the man!' Can you imagine what David must have felt as those words stabbed him in his soul? After all this time his sins had found him out, just as Numbers 32:23 said they would.

When the king heard Nathan's words, he did not need to have the meaning of the parable explained to him. It was obvious to him that he was the rich man in the story, and he knew that Uriah was the poor man. He did not have to be told that he had taken for himself the dearly loved wife of Uriah, even though he had many wives and concubines to give him pleasure whenever he needed it. In fact every single part of this story hit David's conscience and convicted him of his sin, especially those words, 'The rich man ... took the ewe lamb that belonged to the poor man and prepared it [killed it] for the one who had come to him.'

At long last David's conscience had caught up with him. Believers can commit sin just as David did, but eventually the truth will come to light. There are probably very few people reading this book who have never had their consciences stricken because of something they had done wrong. There is a story told about the great Victorian preacher C. H. Spurgeon who, when a very young lad, saw a backsliding Christian drinking in the local ale house, instead of attending church.

Spurgeon is reported to have gone up to the man and pointed his finger at him and said, very sternly, 'What doest thou here, Elijah?' Apparently the man was broken down in tears and immediately left his worldly ways and returned to the people of God.

It was David's restless spirit which had caused him to gaze upon the dearly loved wife of Uriah. It was his unbridled sensuality which had urged him to take Uriah's 'ewe lamb' and 'defile her'. When David took Bathsheba he was not obeying his inbuilt conscience; that would have told him that she belonged to another. He was ignoring the sentiment of Proverbs 4:23, 'Above all else, guard your heart, for it is the wellspring of life.' In the New Testament Paul says a similar thing. He exhorts us to 'take captive every thought to make it obedient to Christ' (2 Corinthians 10:5). We may not be kings or queens, or even very rich, but we can still be tempted by lust. Men of any age can sear their consciences when they gaze at a pretty young woman; women can also be drawn away by the numerous allurements of the flesh. We all need to be on our guard the whole time lest we are drawn away by the enticements of the flesh.

THE CONSEQUENCES OF THE MESSAGE
Before David could repent he needed to have the consequences of his sin brought before him. Sadly it seems that in so many churches today there is little emphasis on what the Puritans used to call 'law-work'. They meant by this that before a person can be restored to a right relationship with God they need to be convicted of the awfulness of their sin. Repentance is much, much more than a person's saying, 'I'm sorry for my

sin'. It cost David a great deal to be brought back to God. He had to be brought very low in tears over the enormity of his sin before he could find peace with God once again. Because we often sin, we need often to come in humble repentance daily and seek to live a Christ-like life.

Immediately after issuing those chilling words, 'You are the man', Nathan reminded the king of all the blessings which God had heaped upon him. Whenever we are feeling low and cast down in spirit, it is good to remind ourselves of all the way in which the Lord has led us in our lives. It is a good thing to, 'count your blessings, name them one by one' and then be amazed at 'what the Lord has done'.[1]

Nathan started at the beginning of David's career and said that God had anointed David king over Israel, and then he reminded him that God had delivered him from the hand of Saul. God had given him his master's house (Saul's throne), and finally, God had given him the house (the kingdom) of Israel and Judah to reign over. The Lord adds, 'I would have given you even more' (12:8).

With so many blessings we would have thought that David would have obeyed the Lord's every word, yet David 'despised' the word of the Lord (12:9). What an awful thing for a godly man to do. If we treat the Lord's word as though it does not really matter, then we are despising the word of the Lord. If we only notice the blessings of God's word and ignore the warnings, we are despising God's word. Let us resolve today to honour, respect and uphold the word of the Lord in everything we do, say and think.

In view of all these things which Nathan outlined to the king, God asked David, 'Why did you despise the word of the

LORD by doing what is evil in his eyes? You struck down Uriah the Hittite with the sword and took his wife to be your own. You killed him with the sword of the Ammonites' (12:9). But before David could even attempt to make any excuse God said, in effect, 'I am going to let the punishment fit the crime.' 'Because you have been very busy with a sword, David, and that, not always in accordance with my will, I am telling you that 'the sword shall never depart from your house, because you despised me and took the wife of Uriah the Hittite to be your own' (12:10). The Lord kept hammering away at this theme of David's despising God. It is no surprise that David was brought to repentance when he realized how angry God was with him.

Like a wise father the Lord did not overlook the enormity of David's sin and he kept reminding him of his use of the sword. David had killed Goliath, but God emphasized that his great sin was that he had struck down Uriah and had taken the wife of Uriah to be his own (12:9–10). As always God's word came true. The sword did not depart from David's house. Three of his sons came to violent ends; Amnon (13:28–29), Absalom (18:14) and Adonijah (1 Kings 2:25) were all killed in gruesome ways.

The Lord proceeds to say, 'I am going to punish you for these things' (12:11–12). David was going to be driven out of Jerusalem by his own son, Absalom, who would conspire to seize the kingdom from his father (15:1–15) and during the time of Absalom's rebellion he was going to take his father's concubines and make sure that all Israel would know about it as he tried to humble his father (16:22).

When any sensible person is given a sharp warning they will take notice of it. This led David to say, and mean, 'I have sinned against the LORD' (12:13). He confessed his sin to the Lord because he knew that only God could do anything about it. He also knew that the only thing which could take away the guilt and power of sin was a sacrifice. But the animal sacrifices of the Old Testament could only cover over the cracks—and then only until the next sin was committed. Sin needs a permanent solution, and that solution is the death of a sinless man. 'God so loved the world that he gave his one and only Son, that whoever believes in him shall not perish but have eternal life' (John 3:16).

David confessed his sin and sought and found God's forgiveness. Have you?

FOR FURTHER STUDY

1. *Why do we find it easier to point out other people's mistakes than notice and deal with our own? (See Matthew 7:3; James 1:23).*
2. *What steps need to be taken to bring about genuine repentance of sin? (See Acts 19:28; 20:21; 2 Corinthians 7:10; 1 Thessalonians 1:9; James 4:9–10).*

TO THINK ABOUT AND DISCUSS

1. *Think of a situation where you have had a difficult task to perform, which needed wisdom and tact. How did the Lord enable you to carry this out for his glory and the benefit of others?*
2. *How has the concern to make the message of salvation understandable to everyone led to a watering-down of the need for heartfelt forgiveness?*

Notes

1 Hymn by **Johnson Oatman, Jr,** 1897. For the words see an old hymn book or www.cyberhymnal.org/htm/c/o/countyou.htm or www.amblesideonline.org/hymns/CountYour.htm

11 David's pardon from God

2 Samuel 12:13–31

Insincerity is one of the curses of our age. People sometimes speak in haste, without thinking, and afterwards they appear to be truly sorry and apologise for their unkindness. However, their subsequent behaviour shows that they are actually uncaring. When these kinds of people speak about confessing their sins they do not always exhibit a truly godly sorrow. It seems that they are more upset because they have been found out rather than because they have offended against God's holiness. The Bible speaks about confession of sin and it means something very much deeper and far-reaching than a mere 'I'm sorry.'

In this chapter we will be examining David's confession. He meant it when he said, 'I have sinned.' He was truly heartbroken that he had committed adultery with Bathsheba and had been the means of the death of her husband.

DAVID'S CONFESSION (12:13A)

After God had spoken to David through the words of Nathan, the king told him, 'I have sinned against the LORD.' All the while that Nathan had been speaking to him David must have felt increasingly uncomfortable. He came to see the enormity of his sin and he realized how selfish he had been. He was horrified at the way in which he had allowed lust to gain the mastery over his life until the time came when he realized that he must do something about his situation.

He could have been angry with Nathan for pointing out his failures. He had the power to order the prophet out of his kingdom but instead he listened to the words of condemnation and he accepted them as coming from the Lord.

When our faults are pointed out to us we are tempted to make excuses or ignore them. It is no easy thing to sit and listen to a recital of the things we have done wrong. We come to accept that it is no use comparing ourselves with others who have done similar wrongs and have got away with it.

As David listened, he became convicted of his sin and he accepted what the prophet had to say. Although Proverbs 6:27–29 was written much later, these words were applicable to David, 'Can a man scoop fire into his lap without his clothes being burned? Can a man walk on hot coals without his feet being scorched? So is he who sleeps with another man's wife; no-one who touches her will go unpunished.' David would have known the prescription for adultery was death, according to the law of God. It seems that he was so sorry for his sin, and so miserable on account of it that he was even prepared to submit to God's sentence of death. This is why he did not just say, 'I have sinned against Bathsheba,' or 'I have sinned against Uriah.' He said, 'I have sinned against the LORD.' This was in his mind when he wrote Psalm 51:3–4, 'For I know my transgressions, and my sin is always before me. Against you, *you only* (my italics), have I sinned and done what is evil in your sight.'

Even though David knew that he deserved to die for his sin, he still called upon God for mercy. He said, 'Have mercy on me, O God, according to your unfailing love; according to your great compassion blot out my transgressions' (Psalm 51:1). He did not want to be saved merely so he could carry on the rest of his life unhindered. He was so truly sorry for his sin that he wanted to make amends for it. He desired to have the opportunity to put matters right and start living for God and for others, rather than just for himself and his own desires.

David made a good confession. He truly meant it when he said, 'I have sinned against the LORD.' But not everyone is so sincere. King Saul, David's predecessor, said similar words when Samuel, God's prophet of earlier days, confronted him with his sin for disobeying the Lord's command. Compare Saul's confession with David's. Saul said, 'I have sinned.' He used the same words as David was to use and he added, 'I have violated the LORD's command and your instructions' (1 Samuel 15:24). When the word of the Lord came to him pointing out that he had not utterly destroyed everything belonging to the Amalekites, he tried to justify his actions. He felt that the sheep and cattle should be saved and he gave as the reason 'so that they can be offered in sacrifice to God'.

Certainly David had also tried to cover up his sins at first, but when God challenged him he stopped making excuses. Saul said, 'I have sinned,' because he had been found out and future events in his life showed that there was no sovereign work of the Holy Spirit in his heart. We are told in 1 Samuel 16:14, 'The Spirit of the LORD had departed from Saul.' He was never the same again.

David must have remembered what had happened to Saul

FACE2FACE: **DAVID**

and he dreaded the same thing happening to him. He was much more sincere in his confession and cried out, 'Create in me a pure heart, O God, and renew a steadfast spirit within me. Do not cast me from your presence or take your Holy Spirit from me. Restore to me the joy of your salvation and grant me a willing spirit, to sustain me' (Psalm 51:10–12).

DAVID'S EXPERIENCE OF FORGIVENESS (12:13B)
As soon as David confessed his sin, Nathan said, 'The LORD has taken away your sin.' Jesus often spoke similar words to those who were in distress. He said to the paralysed man, 'Take heart, son; your sins are forgiven' (Matthew 9:2). To the woman who anointed his feet with oil Jesus said, 'Your sins are forgiven' (Luke 7:48), and his beloved disciple John wrote, 'If we confess our sins, he is faithful and just and will forgive us our sins and purify us from all unrighteousness' (1 John 1:9).

No-one can hope to live for God until they experience the reality of those words. Saul's usefulness to God was finished after the Holy Spirit had departed from him, but he never acknowledged that his days as king of Israel were ended. In fact he rebelled against God's word. That is why he continually fought against David and tried to keep him from taking up the kingdom which God had given to him.

If we are to do anything useful in God's service we have to come to the point which David reached. We may not have committed such dreadful sins as David did but we certainly have no reason to feel self-righteous. All sin is an abomination in God's sight. Sins are not graded into greater and lesser sins (although the effect of sin may be more far-reaching in some cases). We must never delude ourselves into thinking that there is such a thing as 'a white lie'. Everything which infringes God's law is sin. Until we come to accept that 'all have sinned and come short of the glory of God' (Romans 3:23) we can never hear God say these words over us, 'Your sin has been taken away.'

How did David know that God had taken his sins away? He knew because he recognized that God was speaking to him through the prophet. Few people hear the voice of God speaking audibly to them in these days, but God does speak directly to us through the Bible. When the Spirit of God shines upon that word as we read it, he illuminates our hearts and we come to see that God is speaking to us. This happens sometimes when we are quietly reading our Bibles and on other occasions he brings into our minds a verse or passage that we have read.

David also knew that his sins had been taken away because he had an inner assurance that he had been forgiven. In Psalm 32:1–2 we read these words of David, 'Blessed is he whose transgressions are forgiven, whose sins are covered. Blessed is the man whose sin the LORD does not count against him and in whose spirit is no deceit.' Only someone who has experienced the joy of God's forgiveness could write such wonderful words. David had gone through great agony of spirit while he was under the conviction of his sin and he expressed this in Psalm 32:3–5a, 'When I kept silent, my bones wasted away through my groaning all day long. For day and night your hand was heavy upon me; my strength was sapped as in the heat of summer.' In verse 5 he said, 'Then I acknowledged my sin to you and did not cover up my iniquity' (he had been trying to do that earlier). 'I will confess my transgressions to the LORD' and then with great joy he tells us what God did. He almost shouts it out, 'And you forgave the guilt of my sin' (32:5b). It is no surprise that he ends the psalm, 'Rejoice in the LORD and be glad, you righteous; sing, all you who are upright in heart!' (32:11). Now that he was sure of his forgiveness he could hold his head up once again and join the congregation in praising his God, who had forgiven him his sin.

Although death had been prescribed as the punishment for adultery, Nathan said to David, 'You are not going to die' (2 Samuel 12:13b). God graciously took the punishment away which was due to David. He explains this in Psalm 51:7, 'Cleanse me with hyssop, and I shall be clean; wash me, and I shall be whiter than snow.' In Numbers 19 we read that those who touch a dead body have to be sprinkled with water which has been dipped in hyssop before they can be pronounced well again (Numbers 19:18). Although David was not there when Uriah was killed, it was as though his own hand had plunged the spear into his heart. So it was no wonder that David cried out to the Lord to cleanse him with hyssop, and the Lord did, and he was forgiven and cleansed. This was only possible because of what the Lord Jesus Christ was to do on the cross of Calvary 1,000 years later. That is why we do not have to die for our sins if we confess them to him and seek his cleansing.

DAVID'S BURDEN (12:14–23)
Before David could get too excited, Nathan uttered these devastating words, 'But because [of your sins] ... the son born to you will die.' That poor little innocent baby, who was born out of David and Bathsheba's adultery, was destined only to

live for seven days. Quite soon the baby became ill. David loved that child. He had many other children, but that one was very special, yet on the seventh day of his life he died.

On the eighth day of a Jewish boy's life he is to be circumcised and become an inheritor of the covenant of Israel, but this little mite did not live even long enough to receive that token of God's favour. Innocent children suffer for what the parents do. Many babies are born today with AIDS or as drug addicts before they even take a breath. It cuts us to the quick when the innocent suffer for the sins we have committed!

David was very upset by the illness of this child and he pleaded with God for his life. He fasted and went into his house and spent the nights lying on the ground. He refused to get up or eat any food. He was upset by the illness of the child, but perhaps he was mostly in distress because he was to blame. Round and round in his mind must have gone the thought that if he had not sinned with Bathsheba this child would not have to suffer so much. It would certainly have been better for the little one if he had not been born.

However, when the child died, David arose and washed and put on lotions. He changed his clothes and went into the house of the Lord and worshipped God. Now that the child was taken from him he could cease mourning for his sin. He could now worship the Lord with a clear conscience. There are words of comfort here for any who have lost little babies. David said, 'While the child was still alive, I fasted and wept. I thought, "Who knows? The LORD may be gracious to me and let the child live." But now that he is dead, why should I fast? Can I bring him back again? I will go to him, but he will not return to me' (12:22–23). Those last words must mean that

David was saying, 'The baby cannot come back to earth, but when I die and go to heaven, I will go to be where he is.'

David also had other burdens to bear. In 12:10–12 we learn that he would have to continue to live with the sword and he would have many family troubles. This would be very grievous for him to bear and some of these difficulties are listed in the next few chapters of 2 Samuel.

DAVID'S JOY (12:24–25)

David's sorrow is now turned into joy, just as every repenting sinner's sadness is changed into gladness when their sins are forgiven. David and Bathsheba would have another son and this son would be a child of peace. They named him Solomon and we are told that the Lord loved him. Through Nathan the Lord said the child was also to be named Jedidiah which means, 'loved by the Lord'.

We have further information about the baby Solomon in the parallel passage in 1 Chronicles 22:9–10. Here the Lord says, 'But you will have a son who will be a man of peace and rest, and I will give him rest from all his enemies on every side. His name will be Solomon, and I will grant Israel peace and quiet during his reign. He is the one who will build a house for my Name. He will be my son, and I will be his father. And I will establish the throne of his kingdom over Israel for ever.'

DAVID'S TRIUMPH (12:26–31)

Finally David's military prowess was restored to him. At the beginning of chapter 11 we saw him wishing to stay in the luxury of home, rather than go into battle, but now he responds to Joab's call and the Lord again granted David victory over his enemies. He is crowned king of Rabbah as well as Judah.

When we repent of our sins and receive the Lord's forgiveness, we too can once again take our place in the army of the Lord. He will only grant us victory when we turn aside from our selfish ways and seek to honour him.

FOR FURTHER STUDY

1. Study the following confessions of sin, found in the Bible. List the people who demonstrated that they were truly repentant and those who were insincere (see Exodus 9:27; Numbers 22:34; Joshua 7:20; 1 Samuel 15:24; Micah 7:9; Luke 15:28–21).
2. Find some of the very many expressions of joy at being rescued from sin (see Job 33:26; Psalm 28:6–7; Psalm 40:1–3; Revelation 5:9).

TO THINK ABOUT AND DISCUSS

1. Discuss, or think about, the words of comfort and hope you would put into a letter to the parents of a young child who had died.
2. Outline the steps you would take in trying to help someone repent of their sin and seek God's forgiveness.
3. Share an experience of yours where you were disillusioned by life and how you were restored to the joy of the Lord.

12 Where has all the weeping gone?

2 Samuel 15:13–32

This chapter is about weeping, but David did not weep in annoyance; his was a godly weeping. Throughout the whole of 2 Samuel 15 we read a great deal about weeping and all the events of the chapter from verse 13 onwards are enacted in a very dismal atmosphere, at least from the point of view of David and his followers.

THE CAUSE OF THE SORROW

The problem was that David was king, yet his son was seeking to usurp his authority. We can imagine the disappointment that swept over David when a messenger came to him with the news that 'the hearts of the men of Israel are with Absalom' (15:13). Absalom was David's third son. The first one had been murdered by this same Absalom, and the second one had faded out of the picture. So this third son obviously felt that the kingdom would belong to him when his father died but he was impatient. He saw no reason to wait until then before he claimed the throne for himself, so he wheedled his way into the affections of the people and then formed an army to march on Jerusalem.

FACE2FACE: **DAVID**

When he heard about this, David believed that it was better to avoid a battle in the city and possibly cause it much damage so he quickly left it and hurried out of the immediate vicinity. When David departed we read that 'the whole countryside wept aloud as all the people passed by' (15:23). Later on we read, 'David continued up the Mount of Olives, weeping as he went ... All the people ... were weeping as they went up' (15:30).

There is very much to make the whole world weep today. There is so much unkindness, so much ugliness, so much injury done to innocent children, so much neglect of elderly parents, so much greed, so much injustice, so much exploitation of the poor by the rich, and so many people eager to tread everyone else under their feet so that they can get to the top of the pile. In short, there is an enormous amount of abuse of the law of God. People are not only ignorant of the clear teaching of the Bible but even when they do know it they flagrantly ignore it. They do not care whether they insult God or not.

WHY WAS DAVID WEEPING?

He was weeping because Absalom had rebelled again him. His own son, whom he loved, had turned against him and he was sad, because he knew it was his own fault that Absalom had turned out badly. David had not set him a good example and Absalom had killed his elder brother Amnon. David's only reaction was to be 'furious' (13:21). We are not told that he disciplined his son, or counselled him in any way.

I wonder how many parents today just fly into a rage when their children do wrong, instead of bringing scriptural discipline to bear upon them. The Bible clearly teaches that children, and all of us, must be punished for our wrong-doing. However, due care must be given to the child's age and understanding and the punishment should also fit the crime. The parent who is inconsistent in giving out punishment, allowing his child to get away with something on one occasion, and then coming down heavily upon him or her for the same thing at another time, is being unfair and unhelpful to his child. The parent who allows his child to do wrong, unchecked, is being unkind to the child and making a rod for his own back.

Yet David was not only weeping because Absalom had turned against him; he was weeping because he had to leave his capital city. He had fought hard for it. He had brought the ark into it and had set up a special tent for it to reside in and now he was having to rush away from it, leaving everything behind except ten of his concubines who had the special responsibility of looking after the palace (15:16). He probably thought that no one would harm them, but if we look ahead to 16:22 we can see how wrong he was about that.

David was also weeping because he had done so much for his rebellious son. Although he had refused to speak to Absalom after he had killed Amnon, David eventually allowed him to live in the city. In fact, when Absalom returned to Jerusalem he immediately set about making a name for himself. He provided himself with a chariot and horses and fifty men ran ahead of him (15:1). The other sons of the king only had mules to ride upon. God had warned against the Israelites getting horses because horses had to be bought from the Egyptians, and the Lord did not want his people to go back to Egypt (Deuteronomy 17:16).

However, Absalom was not lazy. Verse 2 tells us that he got up early in the morning (before the official judges arrived) and stood by the side of the road leading to the city gate and he ingratiated himself with the people. He did this by listening to their complaints. He sympathized with their problems. He adjudicated on their behalf and invariably told them that it was the other person's fault. He also put it into the minds of the judges that things would be done properly in future. In fact he behaved as any politician does. We are not told whether he kissed the babies, but he certainly 'stole the hearts of the men of Israel' (15:6).

Not only did Absalom patiently spend four years winning the affection of the people, he deceived David by asking permission to go to Hebron so, he told his father, he could worship the Lord (15:8). David did not tell him that he could worship God in Jerusalem as well as other places because Absalom was very crafty. He said he had to go to Hebron because he had vowed that if he were allowed to return to live in Jerusalem then he would go there to worship the Lord in that place.

He was very subtle. He knew that David would be aware of the Scripture which said, 'If you make a vow to the LORD your God, do not be slow to pay it, for the LORD your God will certainly demand it of you and you will be guilty of sin' (Deuteronomy 23:21). Therefore David said, 'Go in peace' just as Absalom knew that he would. When Absalom arrived at Hebron, his birthplace, and ironically the place where David was first crowned king, he sent secret messengers throughout the tribes of Israel saying, 'As soon as you hear the sound of the trumpets, then say, "Absalom is king in

Hebron'" (15:10). Not only did he do this, but he also invited 2000 men from Jerusalem to go as his special guests. However, they knew nothing about his planned rebellion (see 15:11); nevertheless, they became caught up in the rebellion against David.

How easy it is to become embroiled in controversy. Satan makes sure that well-meaning Christian people easily become discontented. They are quite happy until someone starts complaining about the leaders of their church. Then, before they are aware of what is actually happening, they become disenchanted too, and they raise all sorts of objections which had never come to the surface before.

In view of these things we have to make sure that we remain firmly loyal to our King the Lord Jesus Christ no matter how weary we are in the work of the Lord. A rebellious spirit is difficult to control or justify. When it arises pride takes over our lives. We need to see much more humility in the lives of Christian people in these days.

WHAT MADE DAVID'S SORROW MORE INTENSE?

First of all David was sad because many of the people who had been loyal to him now turned away from him. It must have been like a knife piercing his heart when he heard his messenger say, 'The hearts of the men of Israel are with Absalom' (15:13). Think of all that David had done for the welfare of his people and now they had turned against him. They preferred a murderer rather than God's anointed one.

Some thousand years later Pilate was trying to find some way out of sentencing Jesus to death and he thought he had solved his problem by offering to release either Jesus or

Barabbas (who was a convicted thief and murderer). Pilate gave the people a choice: 'Will you have Jesus or Barabbas?' He assumed that they would choose Jesus who had done them no harm, but instead they chose a murderer.

How fickle people are. We need to make sure that we are made of sterner stuff than those Israelites. We never know when a rebellion may arise against God's people and their leaders, such as is happening in many parts of the world in these days. 2 Thessalonians 2:1-4 says, 'Concerning the coming of our Lord Jesus Christ and our being gathered to him, we ask you, brothers, not to become easily unsettled or alarmed by some prophecy, report or letter supposed to have come from us, saying that the day of the Lord has already come. Don't let anyone deceive you in any way, for that day will not come until the rebellion occurs and the man of lawlessness is revealed, the man doomed to destruction. He will oppose and will exalt himself over everything that is called God or is worshipped, so that he sets himself up in God's temple, proclaiming himself to be God.' Because the attractions of the world are presented to us in such alluring ways we must all take great care that we do not become deceived into following a false leader.

The second reason why David was weeping was because many of his subjects had shown him much affection in those difficult circumstances. When he arrived outside the city all his men marched past him. Not only did his own men go with him but there were also the Kerethites and Pelethites as well as the six hundred Gittites who had accompanied him from Gath (15:18). In addition there were a great many of the ordinary people who stood watching this great march-past, and they showed their allegiance to him by weeping aloud for the king as the army passed by.

Not only were there these people but also certain key individuals sided with David. First of all there was Ittai the Gittite. He was a foreigner from Gath yet he refused to leave David and said, 'As surely as the LORD lives, and as my lord the king lives, wherever my lord the king may be, whether it means life or death, there will your servant be' (15:21).

Although David's own flesh and blood rebelled against him, a foreigner, who had come from the country of Goliath, stood by David. This was because Ittai had come to believe in David's God and so he threw in his lot with David. Like Moses 'he chose to be ill-treated along with the people of God rather than to enjoy the pleasures of sin for a short time' (Hebrews 11:25). Then there were Zadok and Abiathar who accompanied David, and they brought the ark of the covenant with them. Although David was very touched by their concern to have the symbol of God's presence with their rightful king he feared for the safety of the ark and asked them to return it to Jerusalem.

There was one more friend who stood with him at this time. When he finally reached the top of the Mount of Olives he found Hushai the Arkite waiting for him. Hushai's robe was torn as a sign of his mourning. He had also put dust on his head for the same reason. Because David was so warmly encouraged by this man's devotion, he sent him back to Jerusalem as a spy to work on his behalf, in conjunction with the priests Zadok and Abiathar.

A third reason why David wept was because his counsellor Ahithophel had gone over to Absalom's side. We do not know why this was, but it is likely that this man was taking the opportunity to punish David because he was the grandfather of Bathsheba, whom David had defiled while she was still the wife of Uriah. That one foolish and selfish act of David's had brought shame on his life and had led to the indiscipline of his children. Even though the king's sin had been confessed, repented of and forgiven by the Lord, the chastisement for it was still having an effect.

The fourth reason for David's sorrow was because of his own sin and it seems that one of the ways that God punishes us is to allow our children to copy our sins. In Absalom's rebellion David saw the fruit of his own sin and disobedience to God's clear command to lead pure lives. As well as weeping, we are told that David covered his head and went barefoot. These things, the torn clothes and dust upon his head, are all signs of deep sorrow for sin and indications of a repentant spirit.

In his sorrow and desire to make amends for his sin David turned to the Lord and prayed. No-one will want to pray in humility unless they desire to honour the Lord. David knew that God had anointed him to be king and, even despite his sin, he was still to remain on the throne. This was because his sins had been forgiven, and he knew that Absalom would never be king in his place. In any case God had told him that his son Solomon would be the one to succeed him and God's word can never be overthrown.

WHEN WILL OUR SORROW BE TURNED INTO JOY?

We, like David, have often sinned and need to repent and make a fresh start. We will never want to do that until we recognize the kingship of the Lord Jesus over our lives. Too often we try to rebel against the Lord and his word. Oh that we would trust God much more when we are passing through the dark valleys of adversity! David wept, and Jesus wept at the grave of Lazarus. We too need to weep for the state of ourselves and our land. God's laws are being flouted every day. In society at large people only pay lip-service to the Christian faith and many think that one religion is as valid as any other. Living in the era that we do, why do we not weep more often and more deeply for the state of our nation, the church and our own families?

These verses remind us of one of the closing episodes in the earthly life of Jesus. David came out of Jerusalem in great sorrow. Jesus left the upper room, on the evening before he was crucified, in a similar state because he knew that he would soon be arrested in the garden of Gethsemane. David crossed the Kidron Valley (15:23). Jesus left the upper room with his disciples and also crossed the Kidron Valley (John 18:1); perhaps it was very near the spot where his forebear had passed over that dark river. David went towards the Mount of Olives as a despised and rejected king. King Jesus went on that same journey knowing that the people had rejected him as their King. However, David had friends with him as he climbed the Mount, but Jesus only had the small band of his disciples to accompany him into the garden. David's familiar friend Ahithophel had left him and joined the enemy camp. The Lord's own disciple Judas had betrayed him into the hands of his enemies. A great number of people sided with Absalom and many of the ordinary people wept with David. But while the general cry against Jesus was 'Crucify him,' there was a small group of those who 'mourned and wailed for him' (Luke 23:27).

It is no surprise that David lamented in Psalm 41:9, 'Even my close friend, whom I trust, he who shared my bread, has lifted up his heel against me.' We too find that sometimes we are let down by our closest friends and we wonder why God allows such suffering to come to us. We can, however, be assured of this: God knows what he is doing. Sometimes he sends sorrow into our lives to punish us, but that is not always the case. Often it is to strengthen us and make us better people that he brings us into troubles.

When will our sorrows be turned into joy? It will be when we humbly cry out to the Lord for restoration and revival. We need to come humbly before the Lord and seek his face. We are far too proud, too puffed up with our own achievements just now. We must remember that those who come to the Lord with a simple, childlike trust will be given the comfort and strength that they seek.

FOR FURTHER STUDY

1. Examine how some of the children of certain biblical characters behaved (see Genesis 26:34–35; 1 Samuel 2:12; 8:3; 2 Kings 19:37).
2. It is not politically correct to smack your child any more. Compare this attitude to that of the Bible (see 2 Samuel 7:14; Psalm 89:30–33; Proverbs 13:24; Hebrews 12:5–6).
3. How can we avoid being caught up in complaining about our employers or church leaders? (See Numbers 16:41; 17:5; Philippians 1:14; 1 Corinthians 10:10).

TO THINK ABOUT AND DISCUSS

1. Talk or think about some of the advice that you would give to an anxious parent whose child has caused him a great deal of trouble.

2. Give an example of something you have worked hard upon and someone else then took control and you were totally ignored. Explain how you felt, what you thought and how you reacted. How did the Lord Jesus Christ behave in similar situations?

3. How would you help someone who feels rejected? (See Isaiah 49:14–16).

13 Suspended between heaven and earth

2 Samuel 18:1–18

Waiting for something to happen can be one of the most stressful experiences of life, particularly if we are waiting in a hospital and wondering whether we are going to be told good news or bad. Our minds can be in turmoil, not knowing whether our loved one is going to be all right or if there are some complications.

In this chapter we are thinking about the final days of Absalom, the rebellious son of King David. At the start of 2 Samuel 18 we find that he had ridden with his men into battle and three separate divisions of David's army were seeking him. The outcome was very bad for Absalom; 20,000 of his men were killed or wounded.

At the climax of that story we find Absalom riding his mule along a track when, as the Bible puts it, 'he happened to meet David's men' (18:9). Of course nothing ever happens by chance; God ordered these events just as he is in control of us today. The mule walked under a low branch of a tree and Abolom's head became firmly jammed in the tree's thick branches. This jolt did not stop the animal. It kept on going, leaving Absalom hanging in mid-air. Tradition has it that he was hanging by his hair, but we are not given those details in the Bible.

ABSALOM'S PRIDE

Absalom had demonstrated that he was a very proud man who cared nothing for the fact that his father was God's chosen king of Israel. Absalom thought he could do a better job as king than his father.

Whenever anyone ignores the commands of God, they are heading for a slippery downward slope. Absalom showed great arrogance when he usurped his father's authority and his behaviour should be a warning to anyone who is tempted to rebel against God's laws. The Lord will ensure that his own purposes are fulfilled regardless of whoever seeks to thwart them.

Another thing that indicates the Absalom was a very proud man was the fact that he weighed his hair after he had cut it (see 2 Samuel 14:25–26). He forgot both that beauty is only skin-deep and also that God does not look at our outward appearance, but at the heart (1 Samuel 16:7).

There are very many people who are in a desperate plight these days, yet they still will not seek help. They just wait for something to turn up. Even in their distress they are not prepared to seek God's mercy and forgiveness. They remain with their hearts and minds stubbornly fixed against God and stay that way until they draw their last breath. In Revelation 2:18–29 we read about a prophetess, Jezebel, in the church at Thyatira who led the people into immorality. The Lord Jesus himself tells us, 'I have given her time to repent of her immorality, but she is unwilling' (Revelation 2:21). Absalom was the same. He had the opportunity and motive for repenting. He probably knew that his father still loved him and wanted to forgive him. He may even have heard about the instructions which David gave to his troops, 'Be gentle with the young man Absalom for my sake' (18:5) but he refused to turn away from his sin.

For a Christian to go into battle against Satan without the breastplate of righteousness is a very foolish thing to do. The Lord has provided believers with the helmet of salvation to protect their head. He has given us the sword of the Spirit that we might fight against our enemies and he has encouraged us to be clothed with the breastplate of righteousness. The person who professes to live a Christian life without availing themselves of these basic parts of the Christian armour is a very proud and foolish man. He is someone who prefers to depend on his own wit rather than make use of God's gracious provision. For a person to go into battle without protection is just showing off. It is as though they are saying, 'No-one will attack me. I am safe because I can look after myself.'

A third way in which we can see the pride of Absalom is because he erected a monument to himself. Monuments are usually put up to a great man or woman who has died but Absalom wanted to make sure that his was remembered so he erected one in the King's Valley where future generations could see it and say, 'What a great man Absalom was to have such a monument as this.' The excuse he gave was that he had no son to carry on the memory of his name (18:18), but his arrogant behaviour ensured that he is not forgotten. It appears that all his sons had died before him.

The sad fact is that he was not buried near this monument. His death was ignominious and he was cut down from the tree and thrown, very unceremoniously, into a big pit somewhere in the forest, and then a large heap of rocks was piled on top of him.

What had Absalom achieved in his life to make him worthy of honour and remembrance? He had killed his brother in a fit of rage. Even though Amnon had disgraced his sister Tamar; it was not for Absalom to take the law into his own hands. Also he had rebelled against God's own anointed king and tried to overthrow him. Proverbs speaks a great deal about disobedient children. In 15:5 we read, 'A fool spurns his father's discipline' and in 20:20 we are told, 'If a man curses his father or mother, his lamp will be snuffed out in pitch darkness' and finally in 30:17, 'The eye that mocks a father, that scorns obedience to a mother, will be pecked out by the ravens of the valley, will be eaten by the vultures.' As Absalom was hanging, suspended between heaven and earth, I wonder whether any of these thoughts passed though his mind.

When the soldiers found him, although he was at their mercy they were not keen to kill him because they had heard David's strict instructions, 'Protect the young man Absalom for my sake' (18:12). However, Absalom, as helpless as he was, was far too proud to plead for mercy and by the time that ruthless Joab came on the scene it was too late.

ABSALOM'S FAILURE

Why was Absalom such a failure? He failed because he usurped the place of God's anointed one. He knew very well that David was the rightful king, but he was not content with being a son of the king; he wanted the highest place and his ambition was to be king over the whole land.

How many people are there today who desire to be in charge of events? They want to do whatever they like. They are so ruthless that they will do almost anything to get their own way. The sad thing is that many of these people are 'sons of the king', i.e. they are Christians yet they are seeking to usurp the place that the Lord Jesus should hold in their hearts and in the church. We should never try to get our own way in the church. It is what Christ desires that matters above everything else. We need to learn to 'do nothing out of selfish ambition or vain conceit, but in humility consider others better than [ourselves]. Each of [us] should look not only to [our] own interest, but also to the interests of others' (Philippians 2:3–4).

A second way in which we can see that Absalom was a failure was by his choice of counsellors. First of all he sought the advice of Ahithophel who had been David's chief adviser, but now he had sided with his rebellious son. This man was a traitor but he gave Absalom sound advice. He said that he should attack while David's men were tired, and their sole object should be to capture David. If this were achieved then David's army would give up (17:1–3), but for some reason Absalom's pride made him seek a second opinion, so he sent for Hushai. Hushai was really a spy sent by King David and he immediately told Absalom that Ahithophel's advice was faulty. Instead he suggested that Absalom should lead his troops personally and pursue David relentlessly until his army had been destroyed (17:11–13). This advice no doubt inflated Absalom's pride and he accepted it. Yet because he followed this counsel he ended up hanging by his head from a tree.

It is certainly right that we should seek advice from others. Even the cleverest among us does not know all the answers. We need help from good counsellors but the wise man is careful of whom he asks advice. The truly godly person is someone who seeks the Lord in prayer regularly. In Proverbs 8:14–17 we read what God says about heavenly wisdom: 'Counsel and sound judgment are mine; I have understanding and power. By me kings reign and rulers make laws that are just; by me princes govern, and all nobles who rule on earth. I love those who love me, and those who seek me find me.' Absalom was foolish to seek advice from everyone except the Lord. When Ahithophel heard that his advice had not been taken, he went home, put his affairs in order and hanged himself (17:23).

Thirdly, Absalom was a failure because he set great store on having a huge numbers of soldiers rather than in trusting the Lord. As Absalom marched into battle he must have thought to himself, 'I am bound to win because I have more men in my army than my father has.' As it happened the battle took place in the forest of Ephraim and, much to Absalom's surprise, he lost an enormous number of men and it appears that many of them perished because they were lost in the forest (see 18:8).

Why did Absalom lose the battle? He went astray because David's men had better leadership and the Lord God was with him and his men.

There are many today who are fighting against the Lord and his ways. They think that just because God's people are comparatively few in number it means that Christians are insignificant. Although the people of the world and worldly systems seem to be winning in the battle of life, it cannot be so in the end. The reason is that God is with us who fight for the Lord and if God is with us at the beginning of the battle, he will continue to be with us right up until the end of our days, and beyond. Paul wrote, 'If God is for us, who can be against us? He who did not spare his own Son, but gave him up for us all—how will he not also, along with him, graciously give us all things?' (Romans 8:31–32).

ABSALOM'S END

Absalom ended up as someone who was fit neither for earth nor heaven; he was suspended between both. What a waste of a life! He rejected his father and his father's authority over him. He not only turned his back upon David, he sought to overthrow his kingdom. At the end of his life he was on his own, just waiting to be finished off! That is how we will all have to die—on our own. Whether we die peacefully or as traitors we will all have to face our Maker and then we will be on our own. We will have to give an account of our lives to the Lord, the Judge of all things. Paul tells us, 'For we must all appear before the judgment seat of Christ, that each one may receive what is due to him for the things done while in the body, whether good or bad' (2 Corinthians 5:10).

Absalom's end need not have been as it was. He still had a loving father. Although he had rejected David, David had not forgotten him. He loved Absolom dearly and when he finally heard that his son was dead, no-one could console him. He wept bitterly, 'O Absalom, my son, my son!' (18:33). David would certainly have forgiven Absalom for all his wrong-doing if only he had repented and asked for forgiveness, but he was too proud and too stupid to plead for mercy. So he died, defenceless at the hands of Joab and his men. What a wasted life!

We do not have to die like that. We have a Father in

heaven who is ready to forgive us. We just have to sink our pride and call out for his mercy. If we come to him like that, we can be assured that he will receive us and welcome us into his family.

Absalom was proud of his own achievements but in Job 20:5–8 we read, 'The mirth of the wicked is brief, the joy of the godless lasts but a moment. Though his pride reaches to the heavens and his head touches the clouds, he will perish for ever, like his own dung; those who have seen him will say, "Where is he?" Like a dream he flies away, no more to be found, banished like a vision of the night.'

Absalom had the opportunity to repent but did not take it. God calls each of us to turn from our sin and 'seek the Lord while he may be found; call on him while he is near. Let the wicked forsake his way and the evil man his thoughts. Let him turn to the Lord, and he will have mercy on him, and to our God, for he will freely pardon' (Isaiah 55:6–7).

The love David had for his son was imperfect; he was but a human father, but the love Christ has for us is rich and free and full.

FOR FURTHER STUDY

1. List some of the dangers of pride (see Proverbs 16:18; 21:4; Jeremiah 49:16; Obadiah 3; Mark 7:20–22).
2. Study each of the pieces of armour in Ephesians 6:10–18 and think how you can use each of these to fight against the enemy of souls.
3. How can we seek wise counsel? (See Job 12:13; Proverbs 8:14–17; Isaiah 40:13–14; Romans 16:27).

FACE2FACE: **DAVID**

TO THINK ABOUT AND DISCUSS

1. What is the difference between being proud of our workmanship and being self-satisfied and boastful?

2. When your last days on earth arrive what regrets might you have? Thinking about them what could you do to attempt to put these things right before you end your days?

3. Talk or think about a time when you felt that you were a failure. How did you cope with it and how did you try to turn your failure into success?

FACE2FACE: **DAVID**

14 A traitor, a cripple and a very old man

2 Samuel 19:20–35

When I taught Religious Education at a comprehensive school, each time we reached the part in the syllabus where Jesus called the twelve, I used to set the children homework like this: 'If you were going to set out to perform a great task, what kind of people would you choose to help you to carry out your objective?' The boys would often give themselves to the job of managing the England football team and they would list the name of the twelve best footballers they could think of. When they did this, I used to say to them, 'No. I don't want their names; I want to know the sort of people you think would be best to build a good football team.'

David had a similar task when he set off to return to Jerusalem to take up the reins of kingship once again. After the death of Absalom many of the people of Judah wanted him to return and reign as king of the whole land. However, not everyone was convinced that he was man enough for the task, and many of them argued about his suitability (19:9–10). Eventually a great many of the men of Judah came to Gilgal to meet David and brought him back across the Jordan and into his capital once again.

FACE2FACE: **DAVID**

The name Gilgal means 'rolling away'. Many years before this God made a fresh start with the Israelites in this very place. It was at Gilgal that all the men were circumcised as a sign that they belonged to God and not to Egypt. The Lord said, 'Today I have rolled away the reproach of Egypt from you.' And the inspired writer comments, 'So the place has been called Gilgal to this day' (Joshua 5:9).

Imagine how David must have felt as he returned after the disappointments and distresses of the previous months. Among the crowd of welcomers were some unexpected people. This group reminds me of the twelve whom Jesus chose to be with him for those three years of his public ministry, none of whom we would have selected for the enormous task of spreading the gospel message.

Among those who welcomed David were Shimei (a traitor), Mephibosheth (a cripple) and Barzillai (a very old man). We will examine each of their characters and see if they tell us anything about the kinds of people Jesus will receive when he comes to reign in all his glory over his people.

SHIMEI

We first meet Shimei in 16:6 when David was fleeing for his life and this man came out and cursed him and all his officials and pelted them with stones. He used very violent language against the Lord's anointed; 'Get out, get out, you man of blood, you scoundrel! The LORD has repaid you for all the blood you shed in the household of Saul, in whose place you have reigned. The LORD has handed the kingdom over to your son Absalom. You have come to ruin because you are a man of blood!' When Shimei said this, one of David's servants, a man called Abishai, said, 'Why should this dead dog curse my lord the king? Let me go over and cut off his head.' However, David calmly replied, 'Leave him alone; let him curse' (16:10–11).

What must David have thought? The rebellion was over and here was this traitor coming towards him to welcome him back into his capital city! I'm sure he was very careful not to say or do anything to arouse the old spirit of mutiny in anyone, so he tried to ignore Shimei and he and his men continued along the road.

If someone had treated me as Shimei had behaved towards David I feel sure that I would not be quick to forgive him and would certainly wait to see if he were sincere in his change of allegiance. So what was the king to do when he saw Shimei coming to welcome him? Certainly Abishai was not happy about the situation, and even if David had forgotten Shimei's appalling behavour *he* had not done so, and he said to his master, 'Shouldn't Shimei be put to death for this? He cursed the LORD's anointed' (19:21). But we see David's humility and gracious attitude when he said, 'Should anyone be put to death in Israel today?' David meant that he did not want anyone to be killed on this day of good tidings. He wanted nothing to spoil its joy.

David did not want Shimei to be killed for political reasons, but also because he noticed that Shimei had undergone a change of heart. It seems that David believed that Shimei had broken with his old way of life and that he now had a completely new attitude. What evidence did David have about the sincerity of Shimei? He not only listened to his words but he noticed his real humility. Humility is in very short supply these days. People are too full of their own importance. They are very reluctant to admit their inadequacies.

It is clear from this account that Shimei had ceased his defiant conduct. The first thing he did was to fall prostrate before the king because he knew that he was not worthy of the king's mercy. Next he freely confessed his sins and did not try to blame anyone else for his wickedness. Instead he humbly asked David's forgiveness: 'May my lord not hold me guilty.' Next he came straight to the point, and talked about the thing which was foremost on his mind and lay heavily upon his conscience. He pleaded with David, 'Do not remember how your servant did wrong on the day my lord the king left Jerusalem. For I your servant know that I have sinned, but today I have come here as the first of the whole house of Joseph to come down and meet my lord the king' (19:18–20).

It was his sin that weighed most heavily upon his mind. Any repentance must start with a clear acknowledgement of our own wrong-doing. Shimei made no attempt to make excuses for his bad behaviour. He knew that the blame lay fairly and squarely on his own shoulders. So often our problem is that we find it very difficult to admit our wrong. However, we must do so if we are to know the peace of God in our hearts and consciences.

So David forgave Shimei and welcomed him as one of his followers. He had no problem in forgetting and forgiving Shimei's conduct and he promised on oath that he would not be put to death (19:23). I do not know whether Shimei ever doubted the king's word. I wonder if he ever thought, 'Well, that's all right for now, but I don't suppose David will remember his solemn promise to me if he gets up in a very bad mood one day and suddenly turns against me.'

How different it is for us when the King of Kings speaks

directly to us and says, 'Son, daughter, your sins which are many are all forgiven you' (see e.g. Luke 7:47). When Jesus impresses upon us, 'You shall not die, but live,' then how can we doubt that he means it? We can have full assurance that God will always keep his promises to us. How wonderful is God's forgiveness of his people. This is the gospel truth, that no born-again believer will die for his sins. This is because Jesus has already done that on our behalf. So God promises us on oath, 'You shall not die.'

By the same token we should be ready to forgive those who come to us and say, 'Sorry'; we should really forgive them. We pray, in the Lord's Prayer, 'Forgive us our sins, for we also forgive everyone who sins against us' (Luke 11:2). Jesus comments, 'If you forgive men when they sin against you, your heavenly Father will also forgive you. But if you do not forgive men their sins, your Father will not forgive your sins' (Matthew 6:14).

MEPHIBOSHETH

We have met this man before too. He was the sole surviving member of Saul's household and he was still alive, mainly because so far as fighting was concerned he was no use, being a helpless cripple. Yet David had showed kindness to him and since then he had a special place at David's table. However, when David was deposed by Absalom, Mephibosheth did not remain faithful to his benefactor. Certainly his crippled state meant that he could not travel with David, yet he seems to have taken a great deal of notice of his servant Ziba who poisoned his mind against David (19:26).

However, Mephibosheth was another person who came to

meet David at Gilgal but what a state he was in! He had not taken care of his crippled feet. He had not trimmed his moustache because it hung down in a very dishevelled manner. Perhaps worst of all he had not washed his clothes from the day the king left until the day he returned safely (19:24).

Was this any condition in which to greet the king? He had let himself go so much because he had been so miserable since David had left. Being of royal blood he could have attempted to take the throne himself but instead of taking advantage of the situation he mourned for David. Like the guests that Jesus spoke of in Matthew 9:15, he was sad.

The only thing that Mephibosheth wanted out of life was to have David back as king and to be at his seat at the king's table. He was not interested in being given back half of his rightful property (which Ziba had stolen from him). In fact he said, 'Let [Ziba] take everything, now that my lord the king has arrived home safely' (19:30). He said to David, 'What right do I have to make any more appeals to the king?' (19:28).

Is that the kind of spirit we have? Are we prepared to sacrifice everything we own, just so long as we can be in the presence of our Lord? That is the mark of a truly holy person. We should seek to spend more time in the presence of the Lord by prayerfully reading and studying his word, the Bible.

BARZILLAI
One of the most remarkable people to welcome the return of his king was an eighty-year old man. He had never been a traitor. He had never failed to support the king and, unlike others mentioned, he had always stood by his lord.

He reminds me of Polycarp, Bishop of Smyrna, who, it is

said, had been a disciple of John the apostle. He forfeited his life at the stake in AD 156. When he was about to be burnt the Roman official felt sorry for him and offered to save his life if he would curse Christ. His reply has come all the way down through the ages as an example of his very strong faith, 'Eighty and six years have I served him, and he hath done me no wrong; how then can I blaspheme my King who saved me?'[1]

When David was fleeing for his life, Barzillai was one of those who brought him bedding and bowls and articles of pottery. He also brought wheat and barley, flour and roasted grain, beans and lentils, honey and curds, sheep and cheese from cows' milk for David and his people to eat. He said, 'The people have become hungry and tired and thirsty in the desert' (17:28–29).

David had not forgotten the kindness of this old man so he invited him to cross over with him and stay with him in Jerusalem, and he promised to provide for him (19:33). But Barzillai answered, 'How many more years shall I live, that I should go up to Jerusalem with the king?' He was not being rude and he appreciated the king's kindness but he felt that it was all beyond him at his time of life. Also he did not help the king merely in hope of a reward. He provided for the king because he was in need, and he honoured and respected him. But all in all he felt that it would be better for him to stay where everything was familiar to him. However, instead of taking up the honour himself, Barzillai asked David to take Kimham with him. Kimham may well have been a son or grandson of the old man. Certainly when David's life drew to its close he urged his son Solomon to show kindness to the sons of Barzillai (1 Kings 2:7).

THE KING OF KINGS

There is a day coming when a much, much greater King will come back to claim his people, the King of kings, the Lord Jesus Christ. When that happens, what kind of people will go out to meet him? More importantly, what sort of people will he welcome and honour? I suspect that there will not be many who are wise by human standards. There will not be too many who are influential in the world's eyes, nor many who are of noble birth. The reason is that God chose the weak things of the world to shame the strong. He chose the lowly things of this world and the despised things—and the things that are not—to nullify the things that are, so that no-one may boast before him (1 Corinthians 1:26–28).

Some of those who will welcome the King and be received by him on that great day will have been traitors to his cause. Some will have been half-hearted in their obedience to his commands. Some will be crippled by sin and evil-living and many will be elderly servants of God who have been faithful to him all their days.

In the kingdom of our God there will be all sorts and conditions of men and women. Is it not amazing that Jesus receives sinners? Yet this is precisely why he came and why he died on the cross and rose again from the dead.

The story in this chapter displays human imperfections. Although Shimei outlived David, David warned his son Solomon not to consider Shimei as entirely innocent (1 Kings 2:8–9 and 36–46). However, in Christ's kingdom there will be no imperfections. This is because the blood of Christ, God's Son, cleanses all his people from every stain.

The story of David's welcoming these different kinds of

people is amazing in its wonderful grace, but how much more glorious is the story of the Christ of Calvary who receives sinners, and even eats with them (see Luke 15:2).

FOR FURTHER STUDY

1. When we are saved we begin a completely new phase in our lives. What changes did you have to make in your lifestyle when you became a Christian? (See Isaiah 65:17; 2 Corinthians 5:17; Revelation 21:4–5).

2. Study the following Bible characters and note the changes that came about in their lives through their encounter with the Lord: Peter (Luke 5:8; Matthew 26:75); Zacchaeus (Luke 19:8); the thief on the cross (Luke 23:40–41).

TO THINK ABOUT AND DISCUSS

1. Think of a time when things had gone wrong in your life and recall what steps you took to make a fresh start.
2. Under what circumstances is revenge acceptable and showing mercy appropriate?
3. Explain to a young believer or unsaved person why we should not do well just in the hope of some reward (See Luke 6:32; Matthew 5:46–6:4).
4. How should Christians be living in view of the coming return of our King? (See 2 Peter 3:11–12).

Notes

1 Quoted in **A. M. Renwick,** *The Story of the Church* (London: IVP, 1958), p. 28.

15 A costly offering

1 Chronicles 21

In the days of the early church it was a costly thing to be a follower of Christ (and still is in some parts of the world). The believers regularly faced deprivation, imprisonment and even death, simply because they were Christians.

If we wish to be effective Christians in our days then it will cost us in time, money and energy and sometimes in being ridiculed because of our faith. While our unsaved friend can lie in bed on Sunday mornings we have to get up and go to church. This means that we have to sacrifice our late Saturday evenings. As God's holy people we also have to give up our indulgence in various ungodly pleasures and selfish desires, but we gladly sacrifice these things because we rejoice in being followers of Christ.

Yet there are some who call themselves Christians who are not prepared for the rigours of the Christian life. They want 'cheap grace' and are not wholehearted in their desire to follow the Lord. Whatever our behaviour it is always a challenge to listen to these words of Jesus, 'No-one who puts his hand to the plough and looks back is fit for service in the kingdom of God' (Luke 9:62).

Those who are only looking for excitement need to look

elsewhere because the Lord wants his followers to be eager to make sacrifices for him and his work. David had to learn the hard way that a sacrifice is something which costs the offerer everything.

DAVID'S PRIDE (21:1–7)
At the beginning of this chapter we see that David had once again become established as undisputed king in Jerusalem. But then, without any prior warning, he gave his general, Joab, the command to go and count all his people. Censuses had been carried out in Israel before, but there had been none since the people of God had been established in the Promised Land. It is a little difficult, then, for us to understand why David ordered this counting at this time. It appears that Joab was not too happy about it, but we are not told why he tried to deter David from this. He reminded the king that he had very many troops and they were all now loyal to him and then, rather diffidently, he asked, 'Why should [you] bring guilt on Israel?'

Not to be deterred, David persisted in this, with the aim of finding out how many fighting men he had at his disposal. This showed David's lack of trust in the Lord to supply his needs and also his pride in wanting to boast about his own achievements. These are two great dangers for all those who are leaders in the church. A new pastor wants to know how big the congregation is, and this is one of the ways in which a church's importance is measured. But God says it is 'Not by might nor by power, but by my Spirit' (Zechariah 4:6) great things will be accomplished.

Foolishly the king did not listen to the advice of his

general. Instead he overruled Joab and for the next few months the numbering was carried out. The result showed that there were one million, one hundred thousand men who could handle a sword, and that did not include the tribes of Levi and Benjamin! The counting stopped before these two tribes were enrolled because 'the king's command was repulsive to [Joab]' (21:6). It would seem that Joab knew that God was with his master and he felt that David did not need to know how powerful he was, so far as soldiers were concerned.

Not only was Joab disgusted, but 'this command was also evil in the sight of God' (21:7). It was wicked because it showed that David was out of touch with the Lord. Certainly we do not read that he prayed about this matter. The danger for us is that if we take any action without prayer and diligent study of the Scriptures then we are likely to be in deep trouble.

David's action shows that he felt that he was not accountable to anyone else. Because he was king over all Israel, he thought he could do as he liked. A wise pastor reminds us, 'If you find yourself in the trusted position of unquestioned authority, be careful. Life on the pedestal is precarious. When you fall from the heights, you not only fall hard, you shatter the lives of those beneath you.' Then he counsels, 'Don't live your life unchecked. Surround yourself with those who put integrity on a pedestal—not you.'[1]

DAVID'S REPENTANCE (21:8–17).

We do not know how long it was before David came to his senses, but one day the king said to God, 'I have sinned greatly by doing this [numbering the people]' (21:8). This was not the first time the king had spoken words like these. After his grievous sin with Bathsheba followed by Nathan's rebuke David had said, 'I have sinned against the LORD' (2 Samuel 11:13). As a result of his deep repentance he received the Lord's forgiveness. Now again, near the end of his life, when he should have learned his lesson we see that he has fallen into sin once more.

We are also foolish. We sin, then repent, and receive God's gracious forgiveness. But before too long has passed we fall into our old ways and sin again. These things show us the folly and weakness of human nature and the wonderful grace of God at work in our lives. We should impress upon our hearts these words which God gave to Solomon, some years after these events, 'If my people, who are called by my name, will humble themselves and pray and seek my face and turn from their wicked ways, then will I hear from heaven and will forgive their sin and will heal their land' (2 Chronicles 7:14).

In his confession and his repentance David asked the Lord, 'I beg you, take away the guilt of your servant. I have done a very foolish thing,' and Gad, whom we last met when David was sheltering in the cave of Adullam, gives him the word of the Lord. David was given three options. God was going to punish him, but he could choose which punishment God should bring upon the land.

David could have either three years of famine, or three months when the Israelites would be defeated by the enemies, or they could have three days when the whole land would be smitten by the sword of the Lord. These would be days of plague when the angel of the Lord would ravage every part of Israel, similar to the angel of death when he passed through Egypt in the last plague before Pharaoh let the children of Israel leave his kingdom.

What an awful choice for David to make. It is no surprise for us to learn that 'David said to Gad, "I am in deep distress."' He did not try to escape from the punishment. The case of Bathsheba had taught him that sin always brings its penalties, as in the case of former drug addicts who become Christians; they may be set free from their addiction, but often they bear the physical marks of their former lifestyle.

The king did not know how to go about choosing the punishment, so he said, 'Let me fall into the hands of the LORD, for his mercy is very great; but do not let me fall into the hands of men' (21:13). David knew that God would do what was best. He had enough faith to believe that whatever occurred the Lord would make the wisest decision. Just as Abraham said, when facing the destruction of Sodom, 'Will not the judge of all the earth do right?' (Genesis 18:25), so it is with us. We often do not know what we should do, especially when everything seems to be going against us, but our prayer should be, 'Let me fall into the hands of the LORD, for his mercy is very great.'

The outcome was that the Lord sent a plague on the land. This resulted in 70,000 Israelite men being killed in those three days of destruction. I wonder how David felt when he saw the effects of his sinful pride. All those new graves were because of his foolishness. We are not surprised to read then, that David called out to the Lord, 'Was it not I who ordered the fighting men to be counted? I am the one who has sinned and done wrong. These are but sheep. What have they done? O LORD my God, let your hand fall upon me and my family, but do not let this plague remain on your people' (21:17).

David knew that he was responsible for this great sadness, just as every Christian leader has to take responsibility for his actions. James tells us, 'We who teach will be judged more strictly [than others]' (James 3:1) and the Lord Jesus Christ tells us, 'Things that cause people to sin are bound to come, but woe to that person through whom they come. It would be better for him to be thrown into the sea with a millstone tied round his neck than for him to cause one of these little ones to sin' (Luke 17:1–2).

David faced up to his obligations, and so should all who have any responsibility in the church of Jesus Christ. We must never lead little ones astray, nor anyone else.

However, the Lord had already stopped the slaughter; he had said to the destroying angel, 'Enough! Withdraw your hand' (21:15) and the place where the plague stopped was the threshing-floor of a Jebusite (i.e. a foreigner) called Araunah.

DAVID'S INTERCESSION (21:18–28)

The Lord instructed David to go up and build an altar on the threshing-floor of Araunah. Obviously this was a raised plot of ground. It needed to be, so that the wind could blow away the chaff from the corn after it had been threshed. David must have been very relieved that God had told him to build an altar, because an altar was where men and God could be reconciled to one another. The way in which man could be united with God was through sacrifice.

David desperately needed to be forgiven for his sin. He also longed that his people should be cleansed from their iniquity, but what he wanted more than anything else was to be at peace with God. The means of achieving this was by sacrificing an animal and grain on the altar. The king lost no time in approaching the owner of the threshing-floor and he found that Araunah was waiting for him. As soon as the king approached him, he bowed down before David with his face to the ground (21:21). He surely would have counted it a great honour to hear David asking for his humble piece of ground so that he could build an altar to the Lord.

Araunah appears to have been a godly man. He was certainly not brought up as an Israelite, because he was from heathen Canaanite stock but the choice of his threshing-floor shows us a number of things. It indicates that even in Israel foreigners were not outcasts. Even a foreigner had rights which must be adhered to, even by such a powerful person as the king. It also shows us the special value of this particular piece of land.

We first encounter this spot in Genesis 22 when Abraham was called by God to go to the region of Moriah and offer up his only son as a sacrifice. This threshing-floor of Araunah was the very same place and now many years later David was about to build an altar and offer a sacrifice to intercede with the Lord and seek atonement for his and the people's sins. In 2 Chronicles 3:1 we read, 'Then Solomon began to build the temple of the LORD in Jerusalem on Mount Moriah, where the LORD had appeared to his father David. It was on the threshing-floor of Araunah the Jebusite, the place provided by David'.

When the Lord Jesus Christ was eight days old, his parents took him to the temple to present him to the Lord. That temple was built on the exact site of Solomon's temple, which had been built on Araunah's threshing-floor. Then, around thirty years later, the Lord Jesus Christ offered up his life as the only sacrifice for sins in a place just a little distant from this spot.

Araunah was very eager to give David his threshing-floor for nothing. He said, 'Take it! Let my lord the king do whatever pleases him. Look, I will give the oxen for the burnt offerings, the threshing-sledges for the wood, and the wheat for the grain offering. I will give all this' (21:23). But David would not do so and told him, 'No, I insist on paying the full price. I will not take for the LORD what is yours, or sacrifice a burnt offering that costs me nothing' (21:24). A couple of verses earlier he had said, 'Sell it to me at the full price.'

David would have nothing to do with cut-price sacrifices. Many years later the prophet Malachi would have to reinforce this when he confronted the people with their inferior offerings to God. God told them through the prophet, 'You place defiled food on my altar. But you ask, "How have we defiled you?" By saying that the LORD's table is contemptible. When you bring blind animals for sacrifice, is that not wrong? When you sacrifice crippled or diseased animals, is that not wrong? Try offering them to your governor! Would he be pleased with you? Would he accept you? says the LORD Almighty' (Malachi 1:7–8).

David, like Malachi, knew that God is a holy God and he will not be trifled with. That is why David insisted on paying the full price for the land. He knew that his sacrifice was no sacrifice at all unless it cost him a great deal.

The sacrifice of the Lord Jesus Christ at Calvary cost him everything. Therefore we should not be content with bringing our 'second-best' to the Lord. He wants to use us for his glory when we serve him. He demands wholehearted obedience to him and his word and work.

FOR FURTHER STUDY

1. How can Christians demonstrate that they have a strong trust in the Lord? (See Numbers 14:24; Psalm 37:5; Proverbs 3:5; Isaiah 38:3; Luke 5:5).
2. Outline the steps given to Solomon by the Lord in 2 Chronicles 7:14, and make a list of the things you can do to maintain a close relationship with God.
3. Study some of the Bible's guidance about giving to the Lord (see 1 Chronicles 21:24; Malachi 1:5–8; Mark 12:41–44; 2 Corinthians 9:7).

TO THINK ABOUT AND DISCUSS

1. What sacrifices are you prepared to make for the cause of Christ?
2. Notice Israel's continual downward spiral into sin, followed by confession of their sin, repentance and then restoration. What can we do to avoid continually falling into sin when we have repented and been forgiven?
3. Discuss the part played by personal prayer, diligent study of God's word and talking to other Christians to help us find God's will for us.

Notes

1 **Charles R. Swindoll,** *David, a man after God's own Heart*, (Insight for Living, 1977), p. 148.

16 Going home

1 Kings 2:1–3

I suppose the one thing we dread more than anything else is the act of dying. In our society it is not fashionable to talk about death. We like to keep it hidden and pretend that such events only happen to other people. Young people particularly do not want to think about their life on earth coming to an end. Some of them do not worry about harming their bodies with drugs and other contaminants. Their attitude is, 'Let us eat and drink, for tomorrow we die' (Isaiah 22:13), but how foolish it is to go through life without making any preparations for the time when we leave this earth.

Apart from the welfare of her family my mother's one big concern was to make sure that there would be enough money from insurance to pay for her funeral. Most people have some kind of funeral plan, but how few there are who prepare, spiritually, for their death. Not so David. When he came to die, he was ready in every sense for his journey from this world to the next. We can see his confidence shining through: 'Even though I walk through the valley of the shadow of death, I will fear no evil, for you are with me; your rod and your staff, they comfort me. You prepare a table before me in the presence of my enemies. You anoint my head with oil; my cup overflows.

Surely goodness and love will follow me all the days of my life, and I will dwell in the house of the LORD for ever' (Psalm 23:4–6).

David was not afraid to die, nor should we be if we trust in the Lord Jesus Christ as our Saviour. For the Christian dying can aptly be described as 'going home'. Peter speaks about our after-life as 'the home of righteousness' (2 Peter 3:13).

DAVID DID NOT FEAR DEATH

When the time drew near for David to die, he gave a charge to Solomon, his son. 'I am about to go the way of all the earth' (21:2). This great saint knew that death is not the end of everything. My atheist friends think that when they die the whole of their life will be wiped out into the darkness of oblivion. Yet that is not what the Lord Jesus taught. He said that death, rather than being the end of everything, is but the doorway into another life. He told us that everyone will go to one of two possible destinations, along the narrow way or the broad way. The narrow way leads to life, and he meant eternity with all the glories of heaven, and the broad way will lead to destruction, with all the pains of hell, to use the terminology of Jesus (Matthew 7:13–14). Neither of these destinations will enable us to escape from reality. Both of them will take us to a life which goes on and on. The difference comes in the nature of that life. Hell is eternal punishment and separation from God and heaven is eternal blessedness.

David had the absolute assurance that when he came to die he would, at long last, be set free from the sin, sorrow, sickness and despair of this earth. He knew also that when he passed through that gateway called 'death' he would discover a place filled with light, joy and the love of God. Each of us should make sure that we are travelling on the narrow road that leads to life, and this can only be found through faith in the Lord Jesus Christ.

David reminds us that everyone must 'go the way of all the earth'. It is not just ordinary people who have to die; kings do as well. He was ready to leave the earth because, despite his many sinful mistakes, he had served God faithfully.

Many years after this event, while he was preaching at Pisidian Antioch, Paul said that 'David had served God's purpose in his own generation' and having done so, 'he fell asleep, [and] was buried with his fathers' (Acts 13:36). We may not be kings, but we are all still called upon to serve God's purpose where we are. We have not been put on this earth merely to please ourselves. Our job is to serve God and sometimes we can do that by taking over tasks that others are doing, and so give them a needed rest.

David also knew the blessings of dying in the Lord. The great hope that David had when he came to die was, 'And I—in righteousness I shall see your face; when I awake, I shall be satisfied with seeing your likeness' (Psalm 17:15). He was looking forward to seeing the face of God. On earth no man can see the face of God and live (Exodus 33:20), but in heaven we will be with the Lord forever. Paul tells us, 'Now we see but a poor reflection as in a mirror; but then we shall see face to face' (1 Corinthians 13:12).

When David was on earth he had everything that he could wish for, but none of these material things really satisfied him. He knew that his greatest joy would arrive when he woke up in glory to see the Lord. John, writing on the same theme, says that when the Lord appears we shall be like him, 'for we shall see him as he is' (1 John 3:2).

We can learn a great deal from David's attitude. Matthew Henry helpfully draws a distinction between 'death' and 'heaven'. He says that none of us should look forward to death, for that speaks of the curse of God, of pain and departing from our loved ones. What we should look forward to is heaven, for that is eternal bliss. It is where many of our loved ones already are, but more importantly it is where our Lord is.

David was not afraid to die because, for him, death was not just an exit from this world; it was an entrance to another and better one. He knew that as soon as he drew his last breath the angels of God would carry him into glory (Luke 16:22). He was certain that the moment his soul was absent from the body, he would be present with the Lord (2 Corinthians 5:19). He had no doubt that his body would rest secure (Psalm 16:9) and on the resurrection morning he would come forth fully conformed to the image of his Saviour (Psalm 17:15).

THE FUTURE OF DAVID'S KINGDOM
When we come to die, we are naturally concerned about the welfare of those we are going to leave behind. This is why David called for his son Solomon to come to his bedside. He wanted to give him his parting instructions. Certainly he was concerned about the welfare of his son, but he was also anxious about the kingdom which, under God, he had established. He knew that the only way in which his kingdom would prosper would be by Solomon's becoming a godly king. Most of the rest of David's sons had proved to be useless, but

God had given him a wonderful promise concerning this son. He was convinced that Solomon was God's chosen successor to him so he said, 'Be strong, show yourself a man' (2:2).

These are very similar words to those which God gave Joshua when he took over the leadership of Israel on the death of Moses. 'Be strong and courageous, because you will lead these people to inherit the land I swore to their forefathers to give them' (Joshua 1:6). Likewise when Joshua came to the end of his days he passed on similar words to his successors, 'Now I am about to go the way of all the earth. You know with all your heart and soul that not one of all the good promises the LORD your God gave you has failed' (Joshua 23:14).

Those who have leadership responsibilities in the nation, the church and the home must take to heart these words. Paul, writing to the Corinthian church leaders, said, 'Be on your guard; stand firm in the faith; be men of courage; be strong,' and then, to make sure that the balance was correct, he added, 'Do everything in love' (1 Corinthians 16:13–14) Sometimes it takes a great deal of courage to do the right thing, but each of us, whatever our task in the church or the family, must be strong and courageous for the truth of God.

David also told Solomon, 'Observe what the LORD your God requires' (2:3). The word David used here does not just mean 'sit down, gaze and admire this wonderful world'. It means 'contemplate and do'. When the Lord tells us to observe his commands, he means that we must understand the value of them and then do what they say.

David describes the law of God in four ways. He says that Solomon must walk in God's ways. The word 'walk' is often found in the Bible. Walking is what we do to get from one place to another. When God says we should walk in God's ways he means that we should follow the Lord's commands, whatever we do and wherever we go. Pleasing God and obeying his word should be second nature to us, like walking.

Not only does David give this general instruction to his son to walk in God's ways, he also tells him to keep God's decrees and commands. These are the commands of the King of kings. When the Lord issues an instruction, then every member of God's kingdom should obey it.

David ends with a promise and a warning. The promise was that if Solomon obeyed God then he would prosper in everything that he did and all the places where he went. The Lord would keep the promise that he gave to David, 'If your descendants watch how they live, and if they walk faithfully before me with all their heart and soul, you will never fail to have a man on the throne of Israel' (2:4). God always keeps his promises. This is the covenant (the agreement) he has made with his people and this is how it applied to Solomon—if he would keep the law of the Lord, then God would prosper him and the kingdom of David would never cease.

Solomon did keep God's law and as a result he did prosper, but only at the beginning of his reign. The snares of materialism and power soon grasped hold of him, and he ended up as a failure, so did that mean that David's kingdom came to an end? Certainly not. This is where we have to consider the warning given by the Lord. It was implied that if Solomon did not keep the Lord's commandments then the kingdom would be taken from him and his descendants.

Sadly Solomon did not follow the commands of the Lord wholeheartedly, all his days. He was led astray from the Lord, and the punishment was that when he died his kingdom was divided. So what happened to God's promise that David's kingdom and his throne will endure for ever? (2 Samuel 7:16). The answer is that David's kingdom has been established as God said that it would, and it will continue for ever. David's Son does reign, he is still reigning and he will continue to reign for all eternity. We are speaking about 'great David's greater Son', the Lord Jesus Christ. His kingdom, a spiritual kingdom, has been established, and nothing can destroy it.

One of my hobbies and enjoyments is to sing in the Bracknell Choral Society. At Christmas 2005 we sang Handel's 'Messiah'. Most people know the Hallelujah Chorus, where Revelation 11:15 is put to music. We are told that loud voices in heaven will declare, 'The kingdom of this world is become the kingdom of our Lord and of his Christ, and he shall reign for ever and ever.'[1] But that is not all. In Revelation 5:10 we are told of God's own blood-bought people have been made 'a kingdom and priests to serve our God'. There is more still. We ordinary men and women will reign with Christ in his kingdom.

Are you certain that when you come to die you will be in that glorious heavenly company?

The only way for anyone to be sure is for them to trust in the Lord Jesus Christ.

FOR FURTHER STUDY

1. Study those Scriptures that speak about the death of those who 'die in the Lord' (see Isaiah 57:2; 2 Corinthians 5:8; Philippians 1:21; 1 Thessalonians 4:14; 2 Timothy 4:8; Revelation 2:10; 14:13).

2. Compare the verses above to those which refer to the death of the wicked (see Numbers 16:32; Proverbs 11:7; Ezekiel 3:19; Daniel 5:30; Matthew 27:5; Luke 12:20; Acts 12:23).

3. The Bible talks about a Christian's life as a 'walk'. Study the following verses and note how the godly person lives his life (see Psalm 15:2; 84:11; Isaiah 2:3; 57:2; Romans 4:12; 1 John 1:7).

TO THINK ABOUT AND DISCUSS

1. Think of someone you know who is heedless of the careless and dangerous life they are leading and discuss how you would challenge them about being ready to meet their Maker.

2. Take David's parting words to Solomon in 1 Kings 2:1–3 and put them into words that your son/daughter or younger friend would understand and want to obey.

3. How do you cope when you realize that you have been given a promise from God's word which does not seem likely to be fulfilled?

Notes

1   **G. F. Handel, E. Prout,** ed., *Messiah* (Novello, 1902), p. 158.

FACE2FACE: **DAVID**

Face2face with Samuel—Encountering the king-maker

ROGER ELLSWORTH

128PP, PAPERBACK

ISBN 978-1-84625-039-2

Welcome to the world of dirt roads and oxcarts, cattle and sheep, sandals and robes! Welcome to the world of Samuel—one of the most important men in the history of the nation of Israel. Samuel was a great prophet occupying a unique position in the history of his nation. For a long time, Israel had been ruled by 'judges', but Samuel ushered them into a new era in which they were governed by kings. However, we are not taking this 'face2face' look at Samuel because we are interested in his historical uniqueness but rather because he can help us to know the God who made us and who has a wonderful purpose for all who live for him.

Roger Ellsworth has served as pastor of Immanuel Baptist Church, Benton, Illinois, for eighteen years. He is the author of twenty-seven books, including *Opening up Philippians* and *Opening up Psalms*.

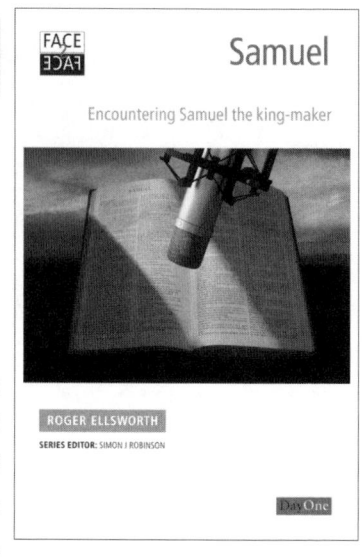

'Roger Ellsworth's book is an extremely relevant and helpful study in the life of Samuel, a much-neglected Old Testament character. It is an extremely practical, pastoral and, most important of all, Christ-exalting-character study at its best and an invaluable addition to a promising series.'
DEREK PRIME

FACE2FACE: **DAVID**

Face to face with Elijah—Encountering Elijah the fiery prophet

SIMON J ROBINSON

80PP, PAPERBACK

ISBN 978–1–84625–011–8

Elijah, the fiery prophet, lived in a time of intense spiritual darkness. People were openly disobeying God's commands, and true worship seemed to have been all but snuffed out. And yet God was still at work! Bringing the power of his word and Spirit into this situation, he used Elijah to break the darkness and to draw people back to himself. This fascinating encounter with Elijah draws out his significance in God's plan and provides us with practical help to live for Christ in the spiritual darkness of the twenty-first century. Each chapter includes questions and points for reflection, making this an ideal book to be used in small groups or for personal study and devotion.

Simon Robinson is the senior minister of Walton Evangelical Church, Chesterfield, England. He has also written several other books, all published by Day One, including *Jesus, the life-changer*, *Improving your quiet time*, *Opening up 1 Timothy*, and *God, the Bible and terrorism*. He also preaches and teaches in Asia and the United States. He and his wife, Hazel, have two sons and one grandson.

'With a pastoral and practical touch, Simon Robinson focuses key incidents in the prophet's life and pinpoints helpful lessons to be learned from his life and times.'
JOHN BLANCHARD

FACE2FACE: **DAVID**

Face to face with David volume 1— Encountering the man after God's heart

MICHAEL BENTLEY

96PP, PAPERBACK

ISBN 978-1-84625-040-8

Raised in obscurity, young David would not have featured on a list of candidates for the future king of Israel-but God had different ideas! Read, here, about how God's magnificent plan unfolded in the life of this remarkable man and in the lives of those around him.

Michael Bentley worked as a bookshop manager and served in the British army before his call to the ministry. He has a diverse background, which includes broadcasting, teaching Religious Education, and holding pastorates in Surrey, South East London, and Berkshire, while being closely involved with his local community. Now retired, he lives in Bracknell with his wife, Jenny, and has five children and six grandchildren. He is the author of ten books.

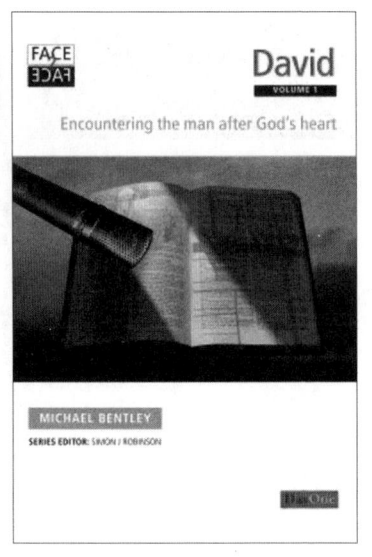

Michael Bentley has an enviable knowledge of the Bible and an admirably simple way of relating its events, and then interweaving the stories with their relevance to our life. Thus, we see how the actions related in the bible can still be appropriate today in the way we live our lives.

FRAN GODFREY, BBC RADIO 2 NEWSREADER/ANNOUNCER

FACE2FACE: **DAVID**